MW00573057

Praise for *Brave Thinking*

"I've been so blessed to not only have experienced Mary Morrissey's work firsthand, but also to have witnessed its impact on countless others. While it seems nothing short of miraculous, it's actually a scientific, repeatable formula that really works!"

JJ VIRGIN, CNS, CHFS, celebrity nutrition and fitness expert and *New York Times*–bestselling author of *The Virgin Diet* and *Sugar Impact Diet*

"In *Brave Thinking*, Mary Morrissey is helping people to upgrade their lives and achieve their goals. She lays out a plan for removing limitations and expanding your creativity and imagination through braver thinking and smarter actions."

JOE POLISH, founder of Genius Network

"Mary Morrissey is the real deal! Her Brave Thinking Tools have helped millions create the life of their dreams. After forty-plus years of deep study into the spiritual side of success, Morrissey has distilled everything she's learned into this indispensable book."

MARCI SHIMOFF, #1 *New York Times*–bestselling author of *Happy for No Reason* and coauthor of *Chicken Soup for the Woman's Soul*

"If you want to learn and be inspired by one of the world's greatest teachers, read this book. Mary Morrissey is a true wisdom keeper, touching the lives of millions, and *Brave Thinking* catches the best of what she knows."

MAYA MARCIA WIEDER, CEO of Dream University and bestselling author

"I believe *Brave Thinking* will become an instant classic that changes how we use our natural powers of the mind. Read this book, absorb its wisdom, and go forward with a genuinely life-changing set of skills."

GAY HENDRICKS, author of *The Big Leap*

"There is no one better than Mary Morrissey to show you a time-tested and proven process that will guide you to create your best life."

CYNTHIA KERSEY, founder and CEO of Unstoppable Foundation

"Mary Morrissey is the Godmother of Personal Development. She has helped millions turn what they first thought were impossible outcomes into fulfilling lives through her simple, reliable, and proven system. All you need to bring is your intention and commitment."

NATALIE LEDWELL, bestselling author and cofounder of Mind Movies

"If you dream of having a life you love, *Brave Thinking* contains everything you need to know. Master teacher Mary Morrissey has written a brilliant book filled with practical and simple steps for those ready and willing to take the journey."

ARIELLE FORD, author of *The Soulmate Secret*

BRAVE THINKING

The Art and Science of Creating a Life You Love

MARY MORRISSEY

PAGE TWO

Cataloguing in publication information is available from Library and Archives Canada.
ISBN 978-1-77458-093-6 (hardcover)
ISBN 978-1-77458-351-7 (ebook)
ISBN 978-1-77458-340-1 (audiobook)

Page Two
pagetwo.com

Haikus by Joe Dickey
Copyedited by Kendra Ward
Proofread by Alison Strobel
Jacket and interior design by Jennifer Lum
Interior illustrations by Brave Thinking Institute
Printed and bound in Canada by Friesens
Distributed in Canada by Raincoast Books
Distributed in the US and internationally by Macmillan

23 24 25 26 27   5 4 3 2 1

bravethinkingbook.com

*To the Spirit of Life who calls us each into greater
and greater life and gives us the total
means by which to cocreate a life we truly love.*

CONTENTS

Introduction

EVERYONE DREAMS, BUT FEW UNDERSTAND HOW TO DREAM-BUILD

---

*"Every blade of grass has its angel that
bends over it and whispers, 'Grow, grow.'"*

THE TALMUD

———————

Accept no limits.

Nothing is too outrageous.

Just . . . what would I love?

———————

Remember How Easy It Was to Dream?

Our imagination was boundless! As young children, we could go on and on about our vision of the future with Crayola-color clarity—the career we would love to have, the house we would love to live in, the places we would love to go, and the amazing things we would do. But as we got older, doubt crept in and those vivid dreams began to fade. Maybe we attempted to achieve a dream but hit a setback and gave up trying. Or others told us we didn't deserve what we desired or ridiculed our efforts with phrases like "good luck with that!" Perhaps the voice that stifled your efforts came from within, telling you that you don't have what it takes.

The good news is that you can learn to dream again and make your dream come true.

Deep inside you is a dream for an extraordinary life. Do you feel like you were made for some special purpose that you have yet to realize? Is there something you have always dreamed of accomplishing? I believe such dreams are not only natural; they are your birthright. You were put on this planet to pursue and achieve your dreams.

To create a life you love, you can't just *dream* it, however; you have to *build* it. My Brave Thinking process is a step-by-step system to banish doubts, resurrect your dreams, and create a plan to go from where you are now to whatever dream life you imagine. Dream-building is my life's work. For the past four-plus decades, I have had the privilege to help millions of people from around the world manifest their dreams.

Most of us don't live a life we love because we focus on perceived limitations: lack of time, limited assets, minimal talents. But our thinking, not our circumstances, holds us back. We are more than mere pawns being moved around on the giant chessboard of life. We are spiritual beings constantly interacting with the energy around us. In this book, you will learn how to harness that energy—what some may call God or Spirit and what I most often name the Infinite—to create big, bold, and exciting changes, first behind your eyes, in the realm of the mind, and then right in front of you.

Dream-building doesn't require a fancy degree or special training. To change your life, you need a vision, a shift in belief, and a set of practices you can repeat every day. The solution to improving everything from your finances to your future begins with an ability to envision a reality different from the one you're already living. When you learn the power of moving from what I call Common-Hour Thinking to a dynamic, bold process called Brave Thinking, everything around you will change.

You've likely been down this road before, having read books on positive thinking or attended seminars on improving your life. You've watched inspiring TED Talks, maybe even gone back to school, but nothing happened. Now, you're tired of hoping. I get it. Your efforts so far have resulted in disappointment and frustration. I've been there, having invested myself in a calling—the ministry—that I thought would last the rest of my life, only to see that dream come crashing to the ground. Perhaps you, too, have been immobilized by a failed dream that broke your heart and shattered your confidence. I know that asking you to risk believing in a better future once again is no small thing. That's why I call this process Brave Thinking. If it didn't require courage, everyone would do it.

I am asking you to trust in a process that has been proven again and again in the lives of millions of people who stood on the same threshold where you now stand.

Take the step and you will view your life in terms of before and after you did.

Blueprinting, Bridging, and Building

There are three phases to building a life you would love.

In part I, "Blueprinting," you will relearn how to dream, and dream effectively, by creating a vision. Before you build a house, you need a blueprint to visualize what your home will look like. What are your dreams? Perhaps you don't know or don't even dare to let yourself think about it. In this section, you will identify where you are in the process and learn to always ask yourself, "*What would I love?*"

In part II, "Bridging," you will use science-based strategies to connect your dream with reality. Before building your dream, you need to systematically expand your thinking to bridge the gap between what you believe is possible and what you truly desire. After all, you don't just want a great blueprint. You want a great life. As your thinking expands, limiting beliefs will fall away.

In part III, "Building," you will learn how to become not only an empowered dreamer but a dream *builder*. This is where you take the tangible steps that ground the dream, turning it into reality.

Each Brave Thinking phase requires tuning your brain like a radio to a channel or frequency of vibration that raises your thinking from the mundane to the extraordinary. You do this tuning by continuously choosing to receive only those thoughts that contribute to building your dream. Such a channel will both *receive* from a Higher Source and *transmit* through your brain and body the thoughts that will transform you and the world around you. Tuning to this frequency brings your dream closer to reality.

If you could add greater fulfillment and success to your life, what would that look like?

Would you improve your health, awakening each morning feeling refreshed and energized? Find your soulmate? Travel to faraway destinations with your loved ones? Perhaps you would expand your business to serve more people and more profoundly impact the world.

Whether or not they realized it, all great athletes, entrepreneurs, and artists have embraced Brave Thinking and seen the results of doing so. This is a book about a growing group of dream builders who are fed up with the status quo, want more from life, and are bold enough to pursue their dreams. *Brave Thinking is a proven, reliable, repeatable system of transformation.*

What follows is an intentional process, and I am careful not to call the people who do this work "dreamers." Successful people are not mere dreamers; they are *dream builders*, committed to the disciplined practice of imagining the impossible and then achieving it. Brave Thinkers know that their greatest control in their life is the power to direct the thoughts that help their dream take form.

I believe in Brave Thinking, and by the end of this book, I hope you do, too.

By using Brave Thinking Tools, you will:

- Come to recognize the deep desires of your heart.

- Break through limiting, self-defeating thoughts into a realm where the impossible becomes possible in the four quadrants of your life—health and well-being, love and relationships, vocation, and time and money freedom.

- Realize that no dream is as great as the person you will become for remaining true to it. Your dream come true is magnificent. The soul that emerges through your journey is greater still.

Brave Thinkers know that their greatest control in their life is the power to direct the thoughts that help their dream take form.

How to Read This Book

Learning how to dream requires you to become familiar with transformational language and apply it to every aspect of your life. You are reading this book because you don't want the next twelve months of your life to mimic the last twelve. To ensure your next year is the best year, you must lean into what I call the three *T*s for a transformational experience.

The first *T* is tune in. Find a quiet place to read this book and apply the lessons, so you can bring your full presence and awareness to what you are learning. The ideal environment is free of distractions, that is, no texting, Netflix, or Facebook, or the best you can muster in this age of constant connection with the outside world.

The second *T* is turn up the volume. More than likely, you have established a way of engaging with learning. You might read books, listen to podcasts, all espousing viewpoints that align with your own longstanding beliefs. As you read this book, I encourage you to try something new. Typical behavior begets typical results, so if you are seeking transformation, you'll want to amplify your engagement. In the seminars I've conducted for decades, I encourage participants to "turn up the volume" on their participation. For your best results, focus on what you *really want* in life. Notice how much it hurts not to get your heart's desire. We'll take a deeper dive into this later, but for now, as you read this book, avoid passive thinking and behavior and you will have better results.

The third *T* is transformational willingness. This is the readiness to let your life be transformed by the dream you have chosen and your decision to pursue that dream. Most of us cling to the familiar. The known provides us a sense of security, even though our lives feel lackluster or unrewarding. Embracing change requires us to venture into the *unknown*, which can be scary. The Brave Thinking Tools provided in this book will guide you step-by-step toward your dream. In this book, I will challenge you to make decisions using Brave Thinking again and again. These decisions will uplift you, empower you, bring good into your life, and into the lives of those you love.

If you are willing to tune in to this present moment, to amplify your engagement, and to make decisions that transform your life, touch your heart right now and say aloud, "I'm in." Does this strike you as a little odd? That's okay. Change can make us feel uncomfortable. But if you don't step out of your comfort zone, nothing changes. So, take a deep breath, and when you're ready, let's begin.

PART I

BLUEPRINTING

EVERY DREAM HOUSE began as a thought in someone's mind. This thought expanded into a detailed vision reflecting the dreamer's values and deep desires. Perhaps there's a suite for out-of-town in-laws or an open-concept kitchen big enough for the entire family to gather for Sunday dinners. An architect captures this vision in a blueprint, that is, a detailed rendering for others to follow in making this home a reality. So it is with dream-building. To manifest your dream, you need a clear vision of how the dream will appear. In the following chapters, you will learn, step-by-step, how to create a blueprint that allows your dream to take form. The blueprinting process empowers you to let go of self-defeating thoughts that stop you from even daring to dream, and to honor the longing and discontent that is calling you to a greater life. In this phase, you will create a vision statement so vibrant that you can imagine yourself already living your dream.

BECOMING A
BRAVE THINKER

*"The future belongs to those who
believe in the beauty of their dreams."*
ELEANOR ROOSEVELT

———————

Dreams are possible

But possible doesn't mean

That they'll be easy.

———————

FROM THE TIME I was a little girl, I dreamed of becoming a teacher. Growing up in an upper-middle-class suburb of Portland, I had an idyllic life with doting parents, plenty of friends, and an adorably shaggy dog. The spring of my junior year at Beaverton High in 1966 promised to be the pinnacle of my high school career: I served as class vice-president, made the drill team, and played the lead in our junior play. To top it off, I was crowned with one of the most coveted of teen titles, homecoming princess.

The world had never disappointed me. I felt invincible, right up until that May, when I realized that I would not be getting my period that month.

Swearing my best friend to secrecy, I asked her to join me for an appointment, made under the name "Mrs. Susan Jones," at a clinic in downtown Portland. I borrowed my dad's Studebaker and, for the first time in our long friendship, my friend and I drove in silence. When we arrived, the nurse instructed me to take off my clothes and put on a smock. She told me to leave behind my clothing and purse and sent me to another room for the exam. Afterward the doctor confirmed I was pregnant *and* that he knew my real name. "Mrs. Jones" hadn't fooled him. He had rifled through my purse and found my driver's license. "You go home right now and tell your parents," he ordered. "Or I will."

This being Mother's Day weekend, I begged him to give me until Monday. When I got home that afternoon, my mother was peeling apples in the kitchen. Turning to greet me, she took one look at my ashen face and asked, "Is something wrong?"

I nodded.

"Did you wreck the car?" she asked.

"I wish that I had," I said.

Marriage was a given. "Abortion," "unwed motherhood"— these words did not exist in our household. Although my boyfriend, Haven, and I did what was expected, my parents mourned me as if I had died. All the hopes they had for me—graduation, college, easing into family life at a more mature age—faded into nothingness.

On May 11, 1966, I became a wife. Wearing a hastily purchased linen suit one size too large, I sat on a hard court-house bench holding hands with Haven as we waited for our marriage license. My mother sat across from us, crying uncontrollably. Haven had just completed his freshman year of college. I was sixteen years old.

Afterward, I went back to school, hoping just to blend in for the first time in my life. But news of a scandal had spread like wildfire through the wholesome halls of Bea-verton High. The same students who had chosen me as a leader now avoided my eyes and cast furtive glances at my waistline. "You must be *really* stupid," a few of my class-mates commented. I told myself that at least I could count on my three closest girlfriends. After all, we'd been giggling and sharing and supporting one another since fourth grade. But their mothers warned them to stay away from me, and they obeyed. As for the rest of my fellow students? They avoided me as if my condition were contagious.

One day, close to the end of the school year, I heard the principal's voice boom over the intercom, calling my name. "Mary Manin, report to my office right away." The principal sat me down and asked, "Mary, are these rumors I'm hearing about you true?"

I said, "Well, if the rumors are that I am pregnant and married in that order, then yes, they're true." He looked at me and shook his head.

Then he said, "You have great honors and terrific academics, but you will not be allowed to return here for your senior year. It would be totally inappropriate for a pregnant girl to get mixed in with the normal girls. But we have a place for people like you if you want to finish high school. You can get a GED. You may even be able to earn a high school diploma. There's a place you can go, not during the daytime, but after dark."

Washington High School was in a part of Portland that I'd never been allowed to drive through after dark. During the day, the building was a traditional high school. But, come evening, it served as the "place" where disgraced girls and delinquent boys were sent to learn. The doors didn't open until seven o'clock at night. As I heard the principal say these words, a burning shame rose in me. I felt my face turn red. Had it come to this? Was I no longer fit to be seen in the daylight?

As my stomach expanded over the summer, I had the prospect of this bleak, nocturnal classroom awaiting me in the fall. Meanwhile, news about my old friends trickled in. They were poring over college catalogs, going to prom, and trying out the latest fad: go-go boots. I wore expandable polyester pants, sensible shoes, and I checked my profile in the mirror daily, trying to convince myself I didn't "show."

That fall, I walked up the steps of Washington High School to begin my senior year, thinking, "Every girl here has a baby or is pregnant. Every guy is some sort of delinquent. This is my new student body." I went to register, and two teenage boys approached me.

One said, "Hi, my name is Paul, but I'm no apostle."

The boy next to him added, "Yeah, I'm Peter and I'm no saint."

I turned to them with my pregnant belly sticking out and said, "My name is Mary. No comment."

So began my senior year. I went to the segregated evening high school, separated from my friends because I had committed the shameful act of getting pregnant. In my sheltered life, I had never even been to that part of town after dark, but now I parked my car and walked five blocks alone in a strange part of the city to study geometry with boys who had been arrested. I feared the shadows on those unfamiliar streets. I feared the delinquent boys, most of whom spent class time making paper airplanes and smirking at the girls. Most of all, I feared the future. What could it possibly hold for me?

And yet, my own dreams stubbornly refused to die. Inwardly I said, "I'll show you." I hadn't abandoned my dream of being a teacher, even though the norms of the times dictated that I could never be one. I had to do something, but what? How could I hold on to that part of me yearning for a greater life when every moment of the day was consumed with earning my high school diploma, navigating marriage, and preparing for motherhood?

Then it came to me. As I was finishing up an assignment for school, I wrote the word "teacher" on a scrap of notepaper and jammed it in my coat pocket. Maybe that sounds trivial, but the act of committing my dream to print gave me hope. Every day I'd reach for that crumpled sheet and gain strength from reading that one word. It felt like I was making a promise—to myself. How I would obtain a high school diploma, much less a teaching certificate, I had no idea. Intuitively, however, I knew something that my mind could not yet cognitively process into words: I knew that without dreams the soul withers and dies.

Some of the girls I attended class with at Washington High accepted their lives unquestioningly. They collected welfare, played with their babies, and boiled macaroni for their husbands. They considered that limited world their lot. I did not, could not, feel superior to them; yet deep down I yearned for something more.

"My whole life hasn't been written yet. I'm writing it now. I can be whatever I want to be. The present does not dictate the future." Or so I repeated to myself over and over as I walked the dark, litter-strewn streets that led to my school, one hand stuffed in my pocket and touching a crumpled piece of paper with the word "teacher" written on it.

That scrap of paper in my pocket grew worn, the letters on it barely legible. But I clenched my fingers around that paper every day. Maybe I couldn't be a teacher right away, but someday. That's how dreams are built. You take a fragment of a possibility and build it thought-by-thought until it becomes a vision. You hold tight to your vision, despite circumstances and other people telling you your dream is impossible. Little did I know it at the time, but my experience as a pregnant teenager was my prelude to becoming a Brave Thinker.

Back then I was not thinking about bravery. I was just clinging to something I cared about deeply that was being wrenched from my grasp. Years later when I told my story, someone commented, "You were very brave." As I thought about that, I asked myself, "What did I do that was brave?" Holding on to a scrap of paper did not fit my definition of courage.

Little did I know it at the time, but my experience as a pregnant teenager was my prelude to becoming a Brave Thinker.

There was no moment of defiance like Rosa Parks refusing to give up her seat on the bus; no transcendence of a terminal cancer patient determined to live each day to the fullest; and none of the boldness of a child who stands up to a bully. Most of us immediately associate courage with action. What I had done was *think* bravely. Behind every brave act is a Brave Thinker, an individual who dares to challenge the status quo and refuses to settle for a little life. It may surprise you, but you have the same capacity for Brave Thinking as those you admire do. Brave Thinkers are not born thinking bravely; they learn how to do this, and so will you.

But rather than a playground bully, the person you are standing up to is you. You are facing down the inner critic who raises doubts and taunts you into submission, giving you a million reasons why you are unworthy of your dream. You lack the money, the time, or the talent. This voice recalls past failures and shameful moments, forcing you to relive them in vivid color. Who are you to even dare to dream? Like a seasoned prosecutor, this voice argues a compelling case against your dream. Standing up to what sounds like overwhelming evidence against your heart's desire takes courage.

You are not alone. Most people don't realize their dreams because they focus more on perceived limitations or present circumstances than on the dream itself. Not so Brave Thinkers.

They are committed to the disciplined practice of imagining the impossible and then achieving it.

Brave Thinkers recognize that they have a power within them that is greater than any doubt or circumstance. They cocreate their dreams with the energy of the universe, what some call God, Spirit, Higher Power, or the term I use most, the Infinite. Brave Thinkers practice telling themselves, "Up until now..." a reminder that their history does not determine their destiny. They honor their discontent, recognizing those inner rumblings as a calling to identify the deepest longings of their heart. They use science-based, universal laws to recalibrate their thinking, shedding old paradigms—views and beliefs about the world and how it works—that distract them from their dream.

Finally, Brave Thinkers understand that fear and failure are an integral part of the process. Without fear, there can be no bravery. Without risk, reward remains elusive. Brave

Thinkers don't let panic derail them. They have a technique to defuse panic and look for the good in a seemingly bad situation. I remember the fear that accompanied me every evening as I walked the darkened streets to night school and as I stepped inside the building, afraid that my life would fall so short of my expectations. But the dream of becoming a teacher was greater. You can focus on your fear or focus on your dream. Focus on your fear and you'll remain stuck. Fear may accompany your journey, but it is not your guide. Brave Thinkers have a clear vision of their dream and are not crushed by failure. They remain open to the unexpected dream, telling themselves, "This or something better."

In fact, I became a teacher, first in the classroom, then from the pulpit, and now around the world, through my Brave Thinking Institute, which reaches dream builders in ninety-two countries. I have had the honor of addressing the United Nations on three separate occasions and the privilege of sitting with the Dalai Lama, Rosa Parks, and Nelson Mandela, asking deeply personal questions. Their responses furthered my understanding of transformation. I have achieved great dreams, but I have also experienced gut-wrenching failure and heartbreak along the way.

Becoming a Brave Thinker—as you are about to discover—requires risks. Think of the next chapter as learning the foundational skill that prepares you for the additional challenges presented in the chapters that follow. For each phase of dream-building—blueprinting, bridging, and building—I provide Brave Thinking Tools. Each tool is an integral part of the process that you return to repeatedly. You might progress toward your dream only to find yourself stuck. That's the time to listen to your still, small voice and perhaps revisit the tool "Begin with the end in mind" to empower you to take that next step, even if it is a baby step. I developed these tools based on various spiritual practices my own mentors taught me, what some of the world's greatest leaders have shared with me, my own life experience, and a pattern I discovered after decades of study that I will share with you in the next chapter.

Bottom line: There are two ways to create your life. One is by design, and the other is by default. If I don't design a dream and a direction for my life, my mind will revert to the default patterns of my previous thinking and shape my reality. Farmers reap only what they plant. Wishing for a different crop is a waste of time. If I plant a pear seed, it will never yield my favorite, Pink Lady apples. If I repeatedly plant thoughts from a history that has not served me well, my history will resurface as my current reality.

None of us knows how much time we have on this earth. Some of us live ninety years of realizing one dream after another. Others live one year ninety times. Regardless of how many years you have left, why not choose that time to realize a life you truly love?

My favorite quote about dream-building comes from Henry David Thoreau. His words are a formula for transformation, and I refer to them throughout this book. Thoreau believed that we are more than the sum of our bank accounts or the level of position we hold and greater than any circumstance we may be facing. Thoreau encourages us to tap into our true source of power, cocreating with the Infinite to "pass an invisible boundary" and "live with the license of a higher order of beings." When you recognize yourself as a cocreator with the Infinite, you have access to unlimited power and a boundless future. Thoreau writes in *Walden*:

> I learned this, at least, by my experiment: that if one advances confidently in the direction of his dreams, and endeavors to live the life which he has imagined, he will meet with a success unexpected in common hours. He will put some things behind, will pass an invisible boundary; new, universal, and more liberal laws will begin to establish themselves around and within him; or the old laws be expanded, and interpreted in his favor in a more liberal sense, and he will live with the license of a higher order of beings. In proportion as he simplifies his life, the laws of the universe will appear less complex, and solitude will not be solitude, nor poverty poverty, nor weakness weakness. If you have built castles in the air, your work need not be lost; that is where they should be. Now put the foundations under them.

In this book, you will meet several of the Brave Thinkers I have worked with who Thoreau would say advanced confidently in the direction of their dreams, and went on to pursue even bolder dreams. These individuals have a great deal in common with you. They know what it means to be lonely, hopeless, doubtful of their own abilities, and fearful of failing—again. Many have struggled to support themselves and their families. Others felt guilty and ungrateful for feeling hemmed in by work that our culture considers prestigious. But they also learned to recognize and honor their inner restlessness that was calling them to a greater life. Instead of settling for mediocrity, they committed themselves to the daily practice of mastering the Brave Thinking Tools.

Among others, you will meet:

- Linda, a feisty former nun who found love in her eighth decade.

- David, who left a secure, but all-consuming, banking career to create a highly successful, six-figure coaching business that affords him the time to take his grand-daughters to school.

- Kim, a former high-fashion model who wound up on the edge of homelessness before employing Brave Thinking Tools. She now lives in her dream home in Florida with the love of her life.

- Lauren, a young woman who felt underappreciated at work and whose husband told her, "You're not my dream girl." Today she owns a six-figure business and is married to the man of *her* dreams.

- Jubril, who was seriously ill and barely scraping by. Today both his health and real estate practice are thriving.

- Nancy, who, on her deathbed, manifested a dream that would live on beyond her.

- Carol, a physician so burned out by her medical practice that she nearly gave it away. Carol sold the practice for over $1 million and now has the time and freedom to live life on her terms.

- Tiffany, once ill, overweight, and deemed infertile, who now is healthy, happily married, and the mother of a daughter she adores.

These Brave Thinkers and others have woven Brave Thinking Tools into their hearts and minds like muscle memory so that when their dream is on the line and a limiting paradigm attempts to distract or dissuade them, they recognize it instantly and send that paradigm packing. The fundamentals are ingrained in them. And their new dreams manifest ever more easily. That same experience awaits you.

THE NECESSITY
OF NOTICING

---

*"What you are aware of you are in control of;
what you are not aware of is in control of you."*

ANTHONY DE MELLO

It's important to

Notice what you're noticing.

Awareness is key.

M Y SON JOHN was born in December 1966, a week before Christmas. I loved him deeply but couldn't help dwelling on past holidays. Life had been so carefree! Back then my biggest worries were finding that perfect trinket for the holiday gift exchange with my best girlfriends and having a date for the school formal. Now I had lost the school I grew up in and the friends who'd been at my side since childhood.

I listened to carolers with a diaper slung over my shoulder, too tired to hang ornaments on the tree. Every morning my husband would awaken before dawn, slip into a pair of white trousers, tuck in his starched white shirt, and try to smile. Then off he went in a converted white truck to deliver bottles of milk on the doorsteps of homes miles and miles away. At night he watched the baby while I attended night school. Haven had dreamed of teaching high school band but had dropped out of college to support our family. His dreams were fading, and so were mine.

In May 1967 I graduated from night school. I still believed that I would be a teacher one day, but in the face of so much disappointment, I didn't always believe in my belief.

"Is this all there is?" I asked myself more than once.

Two months later, I found myself in the intensive-care ward of a Portland hospital, having collapsed with a life-threatening kidney disease. My right kidney, ravaged by a condition called nephritis, was sending waste throughout my body. The other kidney was only half-functioning.

The doctor told me if the blood toxin level in my body could be sufficiently reduced, I could possibly withstand surgery to remove the right kidney.

After that, I would have six months to live.

John was seven months old and had yet to take his first step. Now I might never see him walk. Terrified and help-less, I had nowhere to turn. The God of my upbringing wasn't about to intervene. I grew up believing that when you did something wrong, God got mad and punished you. I had squandered my potential by getting pregnant and kicked out of high school, shaming myself and my family. Even my best friends weren't allowed to see me. And now, I would miss out on raising my little boy, and I was powerless to do anything about it.

The night before I was scheduled for surgery to remove my right kidney, a woman walked into my hospital room and identified herself as a visiting chaplain. She told me that she often prayed for people who were facing difficult surgeries and that my name topped the hospital's list of patients who could use her services. Although I'd grown up going to church, I hadn't attended services for the past few years. And not for a minute did I believe a visiting minister's appeal to the Almighty could do much about malfunctioning internal organs.

But if she wanted to stay with me for a while, I wouldn't object. Mostly, I was scared: it was ten in the evening, my family had left for the night, and I was alone and afraid.

The chaplain scooted her chair up next to my bed and asked me to tell her what had been going on in my life. After I told her my story, she looked at me with compassion and said, "Mary, everything is created twice."

Notice That Everything Is Created Twice

Everything is created twice? I had no idea what that meant. She went on to say, "You already know this. In fact, everybody knows this. But almost nobody knows the *power* of knowing this. The bed you're lying on, the nightgown you're wearing, the sheet covering you, the walls, the ceiling, the floor, all the machinery you're hooked up to. First, these had to be a thought in someone's mind before they became an object. Everything is created twice.

"You already know that if you think embarrassing thoughts, your cheeks get red. If you think frightening thoughts, your heart beats faster."

This near stranger affirmed my feelings, saying, "I hear how much you love your little boy. I also hear how much you've hated yourself lately. You feel deeply ashamed. Could you consider the possibility that the toxic thinking about yourself, the self-loathing, could have something to do with the toxicity that's rampaging through your body and threatening your life?"

"Great," I thought. My bitter thoughts had killed my kidney, and they were killing me. I didn't feel comforted.

Then she suggested that instead of focusing on the past, I could decide something for my future. Whatever I deeply believed would greatly influence the outcome of my illness, she told me. "Can you believe that you don't need surgery and that both your kidneys are fine?"

I told her the truth: "No." Mere words were not going to resurrect a destroyed kidney. Besides, I believed far more in my pain and in the people wearing those white lab coats labeled "MD" than in a stranger who told me I could make a fatal disease disappear.

"Then try this," she encouraged. "Think about the right kidney as the repository of all that is presently toxic in your life. Imagine that when the kidney leaves your body tomorrow, the toxicity that has been poisoning your life will disappear as well. All your guilt and shame about the pregnancy will be removed. With the poison gone, your other kidney will no longer be diseased. Instead of getting worse, you will get better."

I could get better? In this moment I didn't really believe that I could heal, but I could tell that she believed. "Well, I don't know if it's probable," I told her. "But maybe it's possible."

She latched on to that. "That's all we need," she assured me. "There are infinite possibilities in this universe. Just leave one corner of your mind open to the idea that one of those possibilities could occur."

The chaplain remained at my bedside for hours, helping me articulate the new thoughts that would, in partnership with the Infinite, allow me to build the life I wanted to live. We visualized all the toxic shame and guilt being swept into the kidney that would leave my body in the morning, as if a beautiful broom was sweeping away the past. I focused all my energy on this healthy image.

Pause with me here. Why does this matter? Because people in your life right now are telling you what's possible. They look to your current income, education, or health to determine what you can or cannot do. They look to the stock market or the housing market to tell you what you can or cannot have. They believe more in the conditions of your life and the state of the world than they believe in you. But, if you are lucky, you also have someone who sees a power in you that is greater than any circumstance, someone who knows you can harness that power intelligently to create something beyond what ordinary thinkers deem feasible. A stranger intervened in my life. She knew I could heal. She believed in my dreams. And that changed everything.

Before the chaplain left that night, she offered advice that became the basis of my first Brave Thinking Tool: Notice what you are noticing. She predicted that after the surgery, I would, understandably, be noticing my pain from the procedure. "But when the pain of that surgery ebbs," she said, "your mind will want to travel that same well-worn path it's been on the past year and a half. Those toxic thoughts? You'll start repeating them."

She advised me to notice my own thoughts, reminding me that everything is created twice, first as a thought and then in reality. Old habits are hard to break, and I could be totally unaware that my toxic thinking had resurfaced. "You told me that if you could live, you wanted to raise your little boy and you wanted to be a teacher," she said. "Is that right?"

And I replied, "Yes, that's what I would do with my life."

BRAVE THINKING TOOL

Notice what you are noticing

Notice Self-Defeating Thoughts

"Here's what you do," the chaplain said. "After the surgery, I want you to notice whenever a self-loathing thought enters your mind. Then interrupt that thought and tell yourself, 'No, that left with the kidney.' Because we've swept all that toxicity, all that self-loathing, all that self-hatred, all that embarrassment and shame into the kidney that is no longer in your body. But you've got to let it go; it's gone. Keep telling yourself, 'No, that left with the kidney.'"

This was an invaluable lesson. The chaplain went on. "After you affirm that all that shame and embarrassment left with the kidney, immediately imagine holding John's hand in yours. Feel his warm hand. He's five years old. You're walking him into a school and there's a kindergarten teacher waiting at her door to welcome him. Your son is in her class. The teacher is smiling. Your son is jumping up and down. He's so excited about kindergarten. You're happy to be there with him and hug him goodbye as he goes into the room. You head back down the hallway, hearing the *click, click, click* of your heels. As you walk down that hallway, turn left, and there's your classroom. You are a teacher, Mary, and this is your first classroom.

"Then fast-forward in your mind. Now you're sitting in an auditorium, and there's a sea of caps and gowns down on the stage below, and you hear your son's name called. And this eighteen-year-old in his cap and gown gets up and walks across the stage. He shakes hands with the principal, who hands him a diploma. He holds it up high and you feel this immense pride and all the mini-moments of what you did to help him and what he did on his own to culminate in this moment of his high school graduation.

"And then fast-forward. Now you're sitting in the front row of your son's wedding and he's marrying the love of his life. You're the mother of the groom and so grateful to be here."

Then she said a prayer and left my room.

Notice that the chaplain provided me with mental pictures filled with details and emotion. I could truly see and feel myself taking my five-year-old to school and experience the thrill of watching him in the auditorium proudly raising his hand and waving his diploma.

The next morning, I noticed I had slept all night without waking in pain, something I'd been unable to do for weeks, no matter how much medication the doctor gave me. Then off I went to surgery.

A couple weeks later, the doctor visited my hospital room and told me that despite the damage to my remaining kidney, my numbers had stabilized. "You might have a little more time than we thought," he told me, and said I could go home. Haven and John were living with my parents at the time so my mother could help. I went home in an ambulance and was so weak I could hardly lift my head off the pillow. But my numbers not only stabilized. In time, they improved.

Five months later, I met with the doctor, who could not explain what had happened. My kidney was now fully functional. "We're just going to mark 'medical anomaly' on your chart," he said. "Come back in three months, and we'll see what happens." That was in 1967.

Of course, I am thrilled about this result in my life.

My kidney experience became the basis for a lifelong study and practice of transforming lives. I was eighteen years old, young, and hopeful about the future, and this experience gave me the space to think about what I really wanted out of life. My sudden healing felt like a gift I couldn't waste. As the story goes, the Greek scholar Archimedes discovered the answer to a difficult problem while at the public bath. He sprang from the bath and ran stark naked down the street shouting, "Eureka!" Eureka means "I have found it." I felt like I had found a secret to life. Now I had to figure out what came next.

A teacher and lifelong learner

Second only to being a mother, I had always wanted to be a teacher. I went on to complete an undergraduate degree and taught mathematics to children. Later, I shared my story with people of all ages, spending the next four decades studying personal transformation. I read Napoleon Hill, Dale Carnegie, and Norman Vincent Peale. I disciplined myself in the fields of positive thinking, modern physics, psychology, self-help, and personal development. I wanted to give my students the tools they needed to achieve results that exceeded what they thought possible. I started a ministry so that I could help even more people, and this work eventually morphed into an international coaching enterprise that I now share with my adult children. Through this journey, I met many of the world's most influential and successful people across almost every major discipline. For more than forty years, I've been a student of how people transform themselves and the world around them, and through all this study and experience, I have learned a surprising lesson.

The highest-performing people in history all have something in common: their thinking.

There is a pattern to success. Many successful people follow a framework for success without even knowing they are doing so. They don't realize their thoughts and subsequent actions differ fundamentally from the masses. They believe they were in the right place at the right time or attribute success to hard work. Discipline and luck play a role in reaching your goals, but there is more to achieving the impossible than work ethic or happenstance. I have observed that the highest-performing people in history all have something in common: their thinking.

Brave Thinkers notice what they are noticing. In this book, we are working with a proven, reliable, repeatable system of transformation that has always existed. I did not invent it any more than Thomas Edison invented the laws of electricity. I simply discovered an empowering way to use this system. I traveled the world to meet with those who produced extraordinary results with an apparent complete lack of means. Many teachers and mentors have furthered my learning and supported my journey. And after decades of study, I saw a pattern that produces consistent desired transformations—every time, no exceptions, and it all begins with Brave Thinking.

Most people operate in what I call Common-Hour Thinking. Philosopher and author Henry David Thoreau coined the term "common hours" in his book *Walden*. Thoreau conducted an experiment that lasted two years, two months, and two days—living simply and intentionally at Walden Pond in Concord, Massachusetts. There, he spent his time reading, writing, going for long walks, and entertaining friends. He did it so that when it came his time to die, he would not discover that he had never really lived. In his book, Thoreau documented his experience, writing, "I learned this, at least, by my experiment: that if one advances confidently in the direction of his dreams, and endeavors to live the life which he has imagined, he will meet with a success unexpected in common hours."

Understand the Difference between Common-Hour Thinking and Brave Thinking

Common hours are time spent in everyday activities. In our busy lives, we use Common-Hour Thinking, relying on circumstances to make decisions. "Looks like it's going to rain. Better take an umbrella." "The project deadline got moved up. I'll work late tonight and get someone else to pick up Annie from soccer practice." Common-Hour Thinking is essential. Absent the ability to make practical decisions based on existing conditions, life would be chaotic. The problem is that we are lulled into believing it is the only way to think. Common-Hour Thinking is a fact-based, linear way of processing reality that measures what is possible by what resources we believe are available. Common-Hour Thinking focuses on the probable and practical and is constrained by perceived limitations. This type of thinking doesn't require us to observe our own thoughts, which can lead us to be inattentive and unaware that our minds are trotting well-worn paths to the status quo.

The alternative to Common-Hour Thinking is Brave Thinking, which is imaginative, unlimited by time, circumstance, or even the past. Brave Thinkers know that before something can exist in the "real world," it must first exist in the mind. Then, if it's going to take root in life, the dream must be grounded in decisive action. As Thoreau wrote, you must endeavor to live the life you imagine. From there, you can create results that are dramatically different from those in the past, because you are literally seeing the world differently.

Brave Thinkers notice what they are noticing, a process called metacognition, which is defined as the awareness and understanding of one's own thinking processes. It is a common learning technique and meditative practice and can help you get to that creative part of you that can dream and imagine new realities beyond the current one. Call it soul, Spirit, your true self. It doesn't matter. Whatever you call it, you need to develop the part of you that can notice what you are noticing.

Common-Hour Thinking asks, "How can I find my soulmate when I'm working every moment?" Brave Thinking says, "I make time for what's important to me and have all that I need to create a life I love."

For anything to have a chance at becoming reality, you need first to imagine it. When we allow ourselves to imagine a life we would love, we discover resources we didn't know we had. With a well-formed dream, you can advance confidently in its direction. The laws of nature work differently when you are in this state. Take as an example Thomas Edison, arguably one of the most prolific inventors of all time, who aimed to devise a major invention every six months and a minor one every ten days. When asked how he survived 10,000 failures before building the first incandescent bulb, he famously replied that he had never had a failure. He had simply found thousands of ways for it not to work. It was all feedback. "I was never myself discouraged or inclined to be hopeless of success. I cannot say the same for all my associates," he wrote. "Genius is one percent inspiration and ninety-nine percent perspiration."

Imagine our species 170 years ago. If you wanted light after dark, you had to use an oil lamp or start a fire. For hundreds of years, we lived like that. All along, however, the laws of electricity were here, ready to interact with us. We just did not have the awareness to work with them. Edison proclaimed he would accomplish something extraordinary long before he did. He saw it clearly in his mind and made it so. Nothing is more powerful than a made-up mind. Our imaginations are far more powerful than we realize, but we first must learn to tap into them. The power of noticing is how we do this. Whatever image your mind clings to tends to replicate itself in the real world. If you don't claim an idea in your mind, you will never accomplish it. Edison believed that by holding a goal of achievement in his mind, the ideas needed to bring about his desired result would be revealed to him. Using his own version of Brave Thinking, he discovered a formula to realize something that had never existed in the world—a formula that assures that if we wire a light bulb correctly in a house anywhere on planet earth, we will have light. Similarly, you can wire your life to the correct "formula" to build a life you love.

In the previous chapter, I explained how we create results in our lives in one of two ways: by design or by default. If we think the same thoughts year after year, by default, we end up with more of the status quo, no matter how much we might long for something better. Without a new direction, our minds default to creating what they always have. Therefore, we must advance confidently in the direction of our dreams. Creating new results requires learning to partner with the infinite energy that exists everywhere and guides us to produce something we truly desire.

A path to achieve dreams

"Notice what you are noticing" is the most foundational of all my Brave Thinking Tools, and it set Linda Smith on the path to achieve her dreams. The oldest of ten children, Linda grew up poor in Kentucky, wearing hand-me-down clothes from her cousins. There was never enough of anything to go around. Every fall before school started, each child in her family received a new pair of shoes. And every year, her parents prayed that Linda and her siblings wouldn't outgrow those shoes before Memorial Day. "Often, I couldn't take my final exams because I was in a Catholic school that charged tuition, and my dad couldn't make the final payment," she recalls. As high school graduation neared, there was no money for Linda to attend college.

During her high school years, her family's low socioeconomic status affected Linda's self-image, making her think less of herself. "My mother always told me that I could do anything I put my mind to," she said. "Only I never believed her."

And yet, Linda still dreamed of going to college. In her senior year she heard a calling to join the convent and there received an excellent education, earning a diploma in nursing, and, later, three advanced degrees.

Linda remained in the convent for twenty-seven years, even though for the last fifteen, she knew she was in the wrong place. "I was told I had no talent or ability," Linda recalls. "I was expected to be a worker bee." And leaving was risky. As a nun, she had taken a vow of poverty, but the convent had provided food, shelter, and security. Leaving the abbey meant "walking out with nothing in my pocket," Linda said.

But at age forty-five, Linda realized that staying was more painful than leaving, and she eventually ended up in Colorado. Realizing that her mother had been right—she could do anything if she put her mind to it—Linda established her own continuing education program in energy healing and aromatherapy for nurses, which she taught all over the world. Financially, Linda was successful. But over time, her health suffered greatly, and she found herself utterly depleted. One day, while at the airport, flying to yet another city, Linda couldn't remember where she was going. "That's when I knew this chapter of my life was closing," she said. Fortunately, one of the teachers who worked for her offered to take over the program.

Linda moved on. She uprooted herself from Colorado and spontaneously moved to Florida. Once settled, she wondered, "What am I doing here? I'm not a beach girl. I'm a mountain girl!"

"That's when I realized that I had a deep loneliness that had always been there, but I had completely covered it up with constant activity," she said.

Seeking support, Linda flew to Dallas to attend one of my DreamBuilder Live seminars. When she heard me talk about discovering dreams, Linda noticed what she was noticing. She put herself fully in the present moment and admitted, for the first time, that she had a dream for companionship. As a nun and then a devoted career woman for almost twenty-five years, she'd never had a partner and it never occurred to her that she was missing one—until that moment. She had gone out of her way to *not* notice. She went home thinking hard about her dream and some words I shared in the seminar: "You have to take a baby step toward your dream every day."

But how would she accomplish this? Linda didn't go to bars. And she now lived in a state where she knew almost no one. But then she saw an ad on Facebook for a Sarasota singles club and decided that would be her baby step. She paid for a membership and began going on dates. "I wanted to know if the love of my life was out there, if he even existed," she said.

After her third disappointing meetup, Linda was ready to give up. Maybe a seventy-year-old former nun just wasn't cut out for the dating world.

Then on her fourth date, a tall, handsome man walked in and sat down at her table. He had arrived just in time. The two instantly connected and ended up talking all night. Rich was a widower who had lost his wife to cancer. He was devastated by this loss but also felt the same as Linda: that there was a new chapter in his life waiting to be written.

A year later, Linda and Rich were married. At age seventy-two, Linda took Rich to Colorado, her old stomping grounds. Linda's health was no longer an issue. In fact, she and Rich were climbing mountains. Linda even gave me a picture of her and Rich atop the Rocky Mountains at the Continental Divide.

Maybe, like Linda, you wonder if your dreams will ever come true. Brave Thinking reminds you, "I have access to everything I need, and it's never too late."

We live in a spiral galaxy that is governed by immutable laws. Our very DNA is a spiral. Like gravity, there is an unrelenting pull of becoming. We all have the capacity to grow into what we could be. This is life in action. It is the blade of grass pushing through that crack in the sidewalk, stretching into the next version of itself. That bit of green breaks through the cement seeking the light that causes it to grow. This is true for all of us because that same source of life—what I call the Infinite—lives inside us, too.

You feel that pull when you notice and pay attention to it. Notice what you are noticing; tune your awareness to your emotions, thoughts, and bodily sensations. And in that place of awareness, you will be free to imagine a life you would love.

THE NECESSITY OF NOTICING

Brave Thinking Tool: Notice what you are noticing
When you are aware of your thoughts, you can change them.

Teaching points
- Recognize that everything is created twice: first in thought, then in form.

- Notice self-defeating thoughts—and replace them with empowering ones.

- Understand the difference between Common-Hour Thinking (limited) and Brave Thinking (expansive).

FROM DISCONTENT TO DESERVING

"*Twenty years from now you will be more disappointed by the things that you didn't do than by the ones you did do. So throw off the bowlines. Sail away from the safe harbor. Catch the trade winds in your sails. Explore. Dream. Discover.*"

H. JACKSON BROWN JR.

Say, "Up until now,"

And the subconscious sits up

And takes real notice.

WE ALL COME into this life with an innate genius, a daimon as the Greeks call it. We have a life force living inside us, something that gets us up in the morning. But if you are like most people, almost immediately, you begin to pick up messages to play it safe, settle for less. So, you find yourself caught between these two forces— one of pure desire and the other telling you, "No!" Your life energy sends two signals almost constantly: longing and discontent. Both have something to teach you. Opening yourself to acknowledge and examine these inner rumblings is the next lesson in your dream-building journey.

For many of us, the moment we're stirred by restlessness or yearning, we shut down those feelings. As a result, the creative power of the universe doesn't have any room to operate and set free the hidden part of us that is chafing at the bit. The Infinite includes a great life for us, but we need to unbridle our inborn creative energy if we're going to manifest that greater life. Shutting off your yearnings leads to numbing while discontent without direction produces grumbling. Many of our lives are paralyzed by yearnings we refuse to acknowledge or by discontent that festers as anger.

When you think "I wish things could be different" or "I am so tired of this," you are likely discontent, perhaps feeling constricted by life. You long for expansion. Paying attention to this discomfort is one of the first steps to create a life you would love.

Here are three habits that often keep us from examining our longing and discontent:

- Continuing to replay the negative messages we inherited from our upbringing and being lured by seductive tropes that our culture sends us daily.

- Waiting for that day when the kids are off to school, oh yeah, and the mortgage is paid off, and then, of course, when retirement begins. That's when those nagging yearnings and discontent will finally go away.

- Letting past experiences determine the future.

Honoring your longing and discontent takes the discipline of Brave Thinking, because we all inherit fearful ways of thinking that encourage us to conform, play it safe, and shut off stirrings for something greater. For example, if you grew up with a parent who was devastated by the loss of a job that had supported the family, you may unconsciously gravitate to a career with good job security, rather than pursuing the vocation of your dreams. You may have absorbed messages such as "don't trust the government" or "the system has us beat," without ever realizing that how you think determines the life you live. As a child, I wore nice clothes when I went outside to play and didn't scream and yell and romp around the way other children did. My mother was a

Notice your longing and discontent

wonderful person. But having grown up in poverty, she had a scarcity mentality and was scarred by cruel comments made by the kids who looked down on her. To this day, I can still hear my mother's voice warning, "What will the neighbors think?" Growing up I felt a tremendous responsibility to avoid any behavior that caused the neighbors to think less of me or my family.

I was thirty years old before I realized *it did not matter* what the neighbors thought. Furthermore, whatever they were thinking about, it certainly wasn't me. They were probably thinking about their own family, and if anything, worried what our family thought of them.

Your brain is always running a program or two that influences what you can expect from life. Before you begin to dream again, recognize the obstacles standing in the way of what you want. The circumstances of your life don't hold you back, but your belief in their power to do so does.

We often feel disconnected from our dreams. Questioning our abilities, feeling haunted by past failure, or worrying that others will judge us harshly, we may sever ourselves from our dreams. We settle into a comfort zone, where life feels safe, if unexciting. Eventually we convince ourselves that's where we belong. And we keep shutting off that part of us that yearns for something greater. We talk ourselves out of pursuing our dreams or let others convince us to leave well enough alone. Either way, we push our dreams aside and focus on the day-to-day, seeking distractions so that we feel comfortable and avoid the pain of saying no to our dream life.

That's what happened to David Norris, until he looked beyond his present condition and focused instead on what he truly desired. David worked in banking for thirty-five years, a career that brought him wealth and prestige as he turned one of the smallest banks in Texas into one of the largest. David enjoyed a positive work environment and was respected for his accomplishments. He knew that other people would be over the moon to have his job. And yet he felt a tremendous longing and discontent. "I was living somebody else's dream," he said. "This was a good dream, but it wasn't my dream."

David's health deteriorated. He ballooned to more than 230 pounds. He began suffering from debilitating migraine headaches, popping pain medication like breath mints. "I was cutting the pills in half just to make the prescription last longer," he said. "But my longing just got longer."

He felt guilty for not loving a career that benefited him and his family greatly. "I just kept telling myself I was being ungrateful, but I felt so constricted, so restricted," he said. To assuage that guilt, he decided to work even harder, often eighty hours a week. "I told my wife, 'I'm going Lone Ranger,'" referring to the selfless and indefatigable masked hero of television and film lore. Only, as David put it, he became a "grumpy Lone Ranger" who wanted everyone in his life to know the depths of his misery. One day his wife, Candy, reminded him that he was *not* the Lone Ranger. "She said I was more like Silver, the Lone Ranger's horse," David said. "That is, the north end of Silver when he's walking south."

David attended one of my seminars in Los Angeles, but he continued to wrestle with himself. Then he suddenly had a vision of himself leaving the ballroom where I was speaking and arriving at a cold, dark, colorless cemetery with a single grave. The epitaph on the headstone read, "Here lies David Norris. He paid his bills and then he died."

Imagining himself buried alongside his discontent spurred David to acknowledge his longings. He wanted to spread his entrepreneurial wings by building his own consulting business for leadership development. He honored that longing with baby steps.

David began the one-million-step journey of changing his life. It took time and intention, but once he decided to listen to his discontent, to pay attention to what he really wanted, everything began to change. He did not wait for conditions to fall in line.

Guided by a newfound clarity of vision, David created a blueprint for the life he would love, remaining at his job while navigating a gradual transition into building his own business. I worked with David as his company grew and thrived. Today he heads his own highly successful leadership development organization that began with willingness to notice his longing and discontent.

"I'm living the life of my dreams and I have the business of my dreams," said David. "I'm helping my entrepreneurial and business-owner clients raise the lid on their leadership level." His goal: that his clients experience what he has—a life they love.

Notice this: You woke up this morning. Not everybody did. On your own, you don't have that power to wake up and breathe life into your body. Something sacred and wondrous, something beautiful is happening in each of us. It's this thing called *life*. We live and move and have our being in life, and life lives and moves and has its being in each of

us. Our lives are as unique as our thumbprints, each a particular signature on existence. The life force inside you is
forever seeking to grow and expand more fully and freely.
Your discontent and longing are life's way of nudging you,
telling you that it's time to expand. Life wants to be lived
more fully in and through *you*!

We all have a voice inside us that occasionally speaks
up and says, "This can't be as good as it gets... can it?"
The journey toward building your dreams begins with the
uncomfortable exercise of paying attention to signals of
longing and discomfort. This may bring up guilt or fear.
Notice those feelings. Guilt and fear are your old programs
replaying themselves, trying to lure you back into your
comfort zone. When building a life you love, you learn to
let go of the idea that settling is mandatory.

Your discontent and longing are life's

way of nudging you, telling you that it's

time to expand. Life wants to be

lived more fully in and through *you*!

We can either work with life's call, or we can thwart it.
Trying to stop the river of life from flowing through us by
waiting until the timing is more convenient does not work.
Rather, life will find a way to keep flowing, occasionally getting dammed up and distorted into something that shows

itself as pain or difficulty. Most humans wait until something bad happens before they consider changing. Often, this something is an accident, job loss, divorce, disease, bankruptcy, or moral failure. The list is endless. This is life's way of getting our attention, so that we finally tell ourselves, "Things have got to change. *I* have got to change."

Every one of us has experienced those wake-up calls. I certainly have. As C.S. Lewis wrote in *The Problem of Pain*, "Pain insists upon being attended to. God whispers to us in our pleasures, speaks in our conscience, but shouts in our pains. It is His megaphone to rouse a deaf world." Pain wakes us up and forces us to change course quickly, but it is not the ideal motivator.

There is another way to change your life, to live more beautifully and freely, and that is to course correct your thinking before disaster strikes. The voice of discontent is speaking in you right now. You don't have to wait for a crisis to act. The perfect timing is right now. All you need to do is take stock of the areas of life in which you do not feel free and happy then decide you will change what is required to live a life you love. At the end of this chapter, you will find my Life Assessment exercise to identify where you stand in four quadrants of your life:

- Health and well-being
- Love and relationships
- Vocation
- Time and money freedom

Honoring his longing and discontent profoundly affected every part of David Norris's life. As a latter-day Lone Ranger, he used to work up to eighty hours a week, which left each of these quadrants of his life sorely out of balance. Now he works twenty to thirty hours a week, earning far more than he did in the past. His migraines are gone, and his prescriptions have long expired. David has maintained his ideal weight of 175 pounds and calls himself "a lean, serene, Brave Thinking machine."

With his newfound time and money freedom, he and Candy travel the world. His granddaughters adore their "Papa" who picks them up after school and takes them to dance and gymnastics practices, watching as they hone their skills. "We talk together, we play together, we get in trouble together," David said. "But what matters most is that I get to serve as a living example to these girls so that they can grow up and be who they want to be. And that gives *me* life."

This process of assessing your life is not about beating yourself up or wondering what is wrong with you. You've done the best you knew with the support and aware-ness you had at the time. And now your life wants you to expand and go further. Life is always seeking a freer, fuller, expanded version of itself. Ask yourself, "How alive do I feel in my body, my relationships, and my work?" If you're feel-ing restless, that could be the Infinite's voice speaking to you: "There is more to you than you know. Don't settle for a little life." Respect the feeling that is nudging you. The deep longing stirring in your soul becomes a friction that rubs and rubs, creating a divine spark that will ignite your desire into a potent idea.

Use this newfound realization of noticing your long-ing and discontent to do what David has shown is possible. Notice how long your longings have sat with you and what your refusal to pay attention to them has cost you. Acknowledge what you don't love about your life and what you would love. This is the first step to truly transforming your circumstances. And as you notice all this, even noticing yourself noticing it, you can then take the next step toward building your dream.

Listen to Your Still, Small Voice

Another way to honor longing and discontent is to use the help that comes from within, insight that is a gift from our Higher Power, what many call the "still, small voice." This phrase comes from the Hebrew Bible. The prophet Elijah is furious with his people for worshiping the calf-shaped idol Baal instead of Elohim. Nobody listened to Elijah anymore. He had also fallen out of favor with Queen Jezebel, who wanted Elijah dead. The prophet flees into the wilderness, scared and dejected. After spending the night in a cave, he hears God speaking to him: "What are you doing here, Elijah?"

The weary prophet replies, "I alone am left, and they seek to take my life."

God assures Elijah that he is not alone. He tells the prophet to stand on top of the mountain, where the wind is so strong it tears into the mountain, breaking away rocks from the cliffs. Just as the wind dies down, the earth begins to shake. Next, flames erupt all around Elijah. When the flames die down, he hears a still, small voice. Now he understands. God has not been in the howling wind, the trembling earth, or even the crackling fire. Elijah finds God in the silence that ensues once the spectacles cease. He comes to know God in the still, small voice.

Our insight is a gift from the Infinite, not one to be taken lightly. This gift gives us access to great power. This is not a voice that pops up in our mind like a jack-in-the-box; that voice and that power is available to us whenever we choose to listen, and with it, over time, we turn random intuition into consistent, inspired insight. After writing *Madama Butterfly*, Giacomo Puccini said, "The music of this opera was dictated to me by God. I was merely instrumental in putting it on paper and communicating it to the public." The more we listen, the louder and more resonant our still, small voice grows.

By listening to his still, small voice, my son Mat Boggs changed the trajectory of his life. A senior in college, he found himself sitting at his desk one night, staring at two applications. One was for medical school. He'd spent the past four years in pre-med, taking the full slew of courses, including molecular biology and organic chemistry. He had solid scores on his MCATs, and all the medical school recommendations he needed.

The other application was for graduate school in education. In Mat's senior year, he had begun to hear a still, small voice that kept whispering the word "teacher." Being practical, Mat looked up teaching salaries. Immediately he shut down the idea of becoming a science teacher.

But that voice would not let up. It kept whispering to him, "Teacher." He would respond, "Nope. No thank you." And there would be that word again: "Teacher." Finally, he told that voice, "Hey, I talked to you already." But it would not let up.

What happens to a still, small voice when you ignore it? Does it get quieter or louder? Of course, it thunders away at you. Mat couldn't ignore the voice saying, "Teacher, teacher." But he kept pushing it to the side. Although he felt called to teaching, being a doctor checked more boxes for him. He'd still be helping people and making a difference in their lives, plus he would earn more.

So, there he sat, with one application for medical school and another for graduate school in education at the University of Oregon. He called me and said, "I know you've just spent $100,000 on my education over the last four years to prepare me for medical school. But I'm feeling this calling. Would you be mad at me if I decided not to become a doctor and became a teacher?"

All I could do was give him the same advice my father always gave me when I was at a crossroads: "Choose what gives you life."

He later told me that the moment I said that, he crumpled the medical school application and threw it in the trash.

Three weeks later, Mat and I were in India with a group I was leading on a two-week spiritual pilgrimage. Halfway through, on a group tour of a little village, the guide asked if we wanted to meet with a real spiritual master, a yogi who would read our auras. The guide led us through ancient corridors with the scent of bubbling curries wafting through the air and donkeys pushing past us pulling wagons full of cabbage. Finally, we emerged on a rooftop where sat a man dressed all in white with a great shock of white hair. Mat was immediately thrown off because the masterly serene yogi was sitting on an ultra-modern plastic Corona chair. This looked fishy to him. And what if the yogi told him something that planted seeds of doubt in his mind about his decision? Mat moved to leave. I caught his arm and spoke softly into his ear. "Mat, please wait while I sit with the yogi. Then let me share the experience with you."

As I sat down in front of the yogi, he put his hands on my forehead and asked me to close my eyes. The yogi told me he would also close his eyes and then remove his hands; we would both open our eyes, and he would tell me the colors of my aura and what they meant. When he shared the several colors he saw and what they meant, I got chills. He was spot-on with me, and with everyone in our small group.

I told Mat that this yogi was the real deal. My son begrudgingly agreed to have his aura read, as well. He sat down. The yogi put his hands on Mat's forehead, but Mat kept his eyes open. When the yogi opened his own eyes, he said, "Young man, your aura is yellow. Yellow is the color of a teacher. What do you plan on doing with your life?"

Mat's eyes welled with tears and a lump formed in his throat. "I knew that the still, small voice I had been hearing was the voice of my purpose. It was the voice of what was aligned in me calling me to the life I was meant to live," Mat later said. "And I almost missed it by doing what I thought I was supposed to do."

Mat told the yogi, "Well, sir, it's interesting that you say yellow is the color of a teacher because I just enrolled in graduate school to become a teacher."

The yogi took Mat's hand, drew him in close, and looked him in the eyes. "Good job," he said. "Way to listen."

At the time, that twenty-two-year-old had no idea where the brave decision to pursue teaching would lead, that choosing to become a teacher would give him an idea for a book that would later receive a six-figure advance from Simon & Schuster. He didn't know that he would have multiple appearances on the *Today Show*, as well as on CNN. He had no idea that he would go on to develop a multi-million-dollar coaching business, that his reach would stretch beyond thirty children in a brick-and-mortar classroom to more than 100 million people online who wanted to unleash their potential. He didn't know that listening to his still, small voice would guide him to an international speaking career.

That young man sitting at his rickety desk agonizing over the two applications had no clue what was in store for him. He couldn't see the future from his first vantage point, but he is now so grateful for listening and trusting and allowing himself to be led to something extraordinary. It was in his still, small voice; it was in every sign along his path—whether or not he recognized it at the time—that led him to success. That same pull is in you. You feel that pull when you notice and pay attention to it. Wisdom from the Infinite will lead you in your decisions that produce extraordinary results.

We all have access to guidance designed for our needs. As Mohandas Gandhi said, "The voice for truth is available to speak to every single person on the planet, every single day." The voice is available any time you are willing to listen, and it speaks to you through your longing and discontent.

I trust that voice but haven't always heeded what it said. At times my voice would whisper, "Mary, you are not happy," and I was quick to quash that message. Rather than honor my discontent, I buried it, arguing the voice into a quiet corner. At one point, unhappy in my first marriage, I began entertaining thoughts of dying—not because I wanted my life to end, but because a terminal illness seemed like the only "graceful" way to end the relationship! (Even then I was still apparently concerned about "what would the neighbors think?") The source of your knowing voice hears self-destructive chatter like mine but does not condemn or berate you. There's no running tally of mistakes. Instead, it gives you a gentle nudge toward your highest good.

Most of us keep ourselves so busy that we don't pay attention to this voice until we reach a crisis. Without an emergency we avoid addressing the pain. If you've got a cavity, it needs to be filled right away. When the drill nears the nerve, you may wince, but that's also a sign the dead matter has been excised. The living tissue feels the pain. Skipping your dental appointment doesn't make a cavity go away. The longer you put off getting help, the worse the pain becomes. You only reschedule when the ache becomes unbearable, knowing that your dentist will always welcome you back.

Each step that has furthered my awakening has been prompted by the voice within. In a moment of quiet, a warm feeling of insight reassures me, "Mary, this is right for you." Every time I have adhered to my guidance, beginning with "become a teacher," I have grown. Every time I have discredited the voice, I missed opportunities. The voice is available any time you are willing to listen. It has a certain resonance you can feel. Just as you instantly can identify the voice of a dear friend, even a friend you haven't seen in years, you can immediately distinguish the resonance of that still, small voice.

You are worthy of your dream

This chapter is called "From Discontent to Deserving" because Brave Thinking requires another step: recognizing yourself as worthy of the dream you long for. This dream that you envision for your life is a gift. You cannot experience that gift unless you receive it. You may have honored your discontent and acknowledged that the impossible can happen. But until you believe yourself worthy of a great dream it remains out of reach. This section of your dream-building dynamic cannot be skipped. I have known many people who launched a dream without developing a sense of worthiness. Even when they finally attracted into their experience a desired dream, they managed to sabotage it.

We all have these self-imposed limits. We seduce ourselves into ways of living that appear secure, even if they are ultimately very unfulfilling for us.

Many of us have been trained to believe we are unworthy. We may be operating from a paradigm that says something is fundamentally wrong with us and so we do not deserve what we deeply desire. That belief is like a negative magnet pushing away any good we might attract. For instance, we might engage in a relationship but not a deeply fulfilling one. If those we love grow too close, they might recognize that we are fundamentally flawed, so we unconsciously push them away before they can find out. Similarly, we may fail to fully express our talent. Taking risks in a career makes us vulnerable to error, and we fear that stumbling will expose us as phonies. We become so careful, so fearful of mistakes, that we remain on a short leash, never venturing into a realm wherein our greater life resides. This is a very draining, diminishing, and frightening version of life.

Your history does not
determine your destiny.

Many of us define ourselves by our past: Who we are is what has happened to us. "My husband left me; therefore, I am not worthy." "I worked for years to become an engineer, so I can never leave my job." "I became pregnant at age sixteen; therefore, I cannot have a successful career." Past and present circumstances influence us—sometimes they may seem almost to crush us—but they do not have to determine our lives. We always have choices, yet we limit ourselves and our life experience by consenting to conditions. We truly have the power within us to say no to past or present particulars and to allow a new dream to manifest in our lives. Build your dream on a solid foundation of believing. Your history does not determine your destiny.

You may have been raised with hardship. Circumstances in your present life may make it easy to stay trapped. Practice telling yourself this: "Yes, bad things happened in my life, but I am free to choose again. I am free as soon as I acknowledge that the past does not have to dictate my future. I am free to renew my mind, if I simply choose to do so."

I heard a story that reminds me to let go of the past. Eight golfers go out to the fairway and break up into foursomes. The first group plays eighteen holes, then sits in the clubhouse waiting for the other golfers to return. It seems like they wait forever. Finally, here come three men from the second group. These guys are disheveled, just a total wreck. One of the golfers who'd been waiting at the clubhouse asks, "My gosh, what happened to you guys?"

One of them responds, "Oh, it was just awful. On the second hole, Harry had a heart attack. After that, it was hit the ball and drag Harry... Hit the ball and drag Harry."

So, who is Harry? Quite simply, Harry is our deadweight.

We have parts of ourselves that we have long since needed to discard. They have died, but we're still hanging on. We are still dragging our childhood story. We are still hauling around what our spouse did yesterday or ten years ago. We are still lugging the notion that we are not lovable. We are still dragging limiting ideas.

Tell Yourself, "Up Until Now..."

Opening up to dreaming means growing our awareness. We can catch ourselves in limiting thoughts, such as "what I want cannot happen because I don't have a degree." Whenever you find a limiting belief interfering with a desire or a dream, redirect your thinking. If you feel blocked, pause. Ask yourself, "But what if I could?" Otherwise, you'll only repeat your history again.

Then say to yourself, "Up until now..." For example, "As a child, I was abandoned by my mother. Up until now, I thought I was unlovable. Now I recognize that I am worthy of love and the partner of my dreams."

Up until now... David Norris felt ashamed for disliking a career that had brought him wealth and prestige, even though his job made him physically ill. Now he is healthy and the head of his own thriving company.

Up until now... Former nun Linda Smith covered her loneliness with activity. Now in her seventies, she has a life partner who climbs mountains with her.

Up until now... I was a teenage parent with a limited education, and I doubted my abilities. "Teen mother," "the scandal of Beaverton High School"—those titles belonged to the past; they did not have to ordain the future. And they have not.

Many years ago, when I was minister, a congregant named Janice reached out to me. She deeply regretted her lack of formal education. "Even though I'd love to, it is too late to go to school now," she told me. "I'm forty-two years old; if I go to school now, I'll be forty-six when I finish my education."

I asked, "How old will you be in four years if you don't go to school?"

"I don't know what you mean."

"What is your dream? Where do you want to be in your life in four years? Imagine you could start fresh, with no limits, what would you do?"

"Well, I'd begin to look at some colleges."

Janice enrolled in a local community college part time. She did not sign up for a full course load; that was too scary for her. But she did enroll in a few classes and became hooked. She finally realized that her lack of a diploma did not prevent her from pursuing one now. Janice changed the course of her life by telling herself, "Up until now..."

"Up until now, I believed that school was out of the picture for me. Now I believe..."

St. Francis of Assisi, who had grown up wealthy and indulged in all the vices young men of his time indulged in, was once asked by one of his companions, "Why you, Francis? Why did God choose you as a lighthouse to bless the world?"

St. Francis smiled and replied, "Why me? I'll tell you why me. Because there could hardly be anyone who has made as many mistakes as I have. I have done and been everything you can think of that is abhorrent and unholy. I had absolutely nothing to offer the world. That is precisely why God chose me to offer hope to people who feel they have nothing to give, for if the Holy Spirit can work through me, it can work through anyone."

You cannot undo what has already been done. But you can become bigger than the tragedy that befell you by accessing unlimited power from the Infinite. Creators free themselves for a life of abundance, confident they are worthy of their dream.

Grace is a gift of the universe. You cannot earn it. You are born deserving it. Want to know whether you are worthy? If you are still breathing, the answer is that you are. This precious gift of life is yours to live abundantly.

Saying to yourself "I'm too fat, too ugly, too dull, too uneducated to be granted my heart's desire" will result in a self-fulfilling prophecy. You were born worthy. Honor and recognize your true self—and the universe will respond in kind.

That is the message behind one of my favorite stories, which comes from India. A tigress, pregnant and starving, spies a herd of goats in the distance and moves in for the attack. But she doesn't get far. Exhausted, she collapses, gives birth to her cub, and then dies. When the goats return to their field, they find the helpless cub and decide to adopt him. He grows up bleating, eating grass, and occasionally butting heads with his brethren. One day a large male tiger pounces on the goats, sending them scattering. The young cub, however, stays put, recognizing something familiar about the larger animal. Amazed, the adult tiger asks if the cub lives with the goats.

"*Maaaa*," bleats the little tiger.

The adult tiger is mortified at this poor specimen of his species. The little guy, embarrassed, keeps bleating and nibbling grass. So the big tiger brings him to a still pond, where the cub sees his own face for the first time.

"You're no goat," the big tiger tells him. "You're a tiger, like me." The adult tiger leads the little fellow to a den and offers him the remains of a recently slaughtered gazelle.

"No, thanks," the little one says. "I'm a vegetarian."

"Nonsense," says the big guy, and he shoves a chunk of meat down the tiger's throat. At first, the little tiger gags. But after the meat gets into his system, he stretches, bares his teeth, and for the first time, lets out a tiny roar. Then he and his new pal go hunting.

Many of us are tigers living as goats.

Up until now. That first roar, your roar of awakening, is yours to take.

Often your history has formed a limited idea of who you are and what you can accomplish. But if you quiet your mind, you can begin to sense your divine self, that part in you that yearns to roar. Don't allow fear or "I should have" or the belief that "it can't be" drive a wedge between you and your desire. If you do what you've always done, you'll get the results you've always gotten. You'll hear the old chatter that dictates every reason for not taking a risk.

Listen, then pause. Don't let that old chatter block you from tasting your greater identity. Open your mind and roar triumphantly, celebrating the possibilities that exist inside you. No matter what is happening in your life, it is always too early to abandon hope, too early to relinquish the daily practice of cultivating a mindset of worthiness that can transform your life. Your history does not determine your destiny unless you decide it does. You free yourself from the past when you dare to roar, "Up until now..." All your disappointments and regrets belong to a time that is ending at this moment. Let out your yearnings in a first roar of awakening.

EXERCISE: Life Assessment

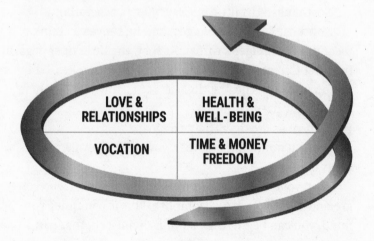

Part of building a dream is honestly assessing the present state of your life. You might not have identified your dream, but you have honored your longing and discontent and recognize yourself as worthy of a life you love. You might be someone with lots of ideas, but you don't know where to begin or which one to choose. You might be afraid to focus on just one dream, for fear of missing out, that you'll be letting the other dreams drift away. Wherever you are, no matter what the dream is or could be, *this is the perfect place to start.*

A simple way to begin changing your life is to *not* erratically change things without any clear direction or focus. All you need to do is take a good look at your current circumstances—what about your life do you love and what do you not love?

There are four major areas in life where you currently have results: health and well-being, love and relationships, vocation, and time and money freedom. To have a successful and fulfilling life, you need to look at each of these areas honestly. So, let's start with the most personal: *you*. Absent good health, life can be short-lived and unnecessarily painful, so part of building a dream life begins with your own well-being. Here's an exercise that can help.

Health and well-being

On a blank page, write "Health and Well-Being" at the top.

Then, apply the Brave Thinking Tools you have learned thus far. Notice what you are noticing and honor your longing and discontent, the inner rumblings that are calling you to a greater life. Pause for a moment and notice if you want to transform something in your health. It could be your blood pressure, stamina, strength, weight, or emotional well-being. Imagine how much easier and better life would be if you could feel vitality in every area of your health and well-being. If you enjoy relatively good health and are free of worrying symptoms, focus in instead on feeling more vibrant and alive. You are looking at ways you can live your life at its best when it comes to your well-being. Could you use some more energy? Get better sleep? Rid yourself of those migraines? Tune in to the areas of discontentment you desire to change and notice your longing there. Nobody needs to see or know this but you, so be 100 percent honest with yourself. This is going to be the framework from which you begin to build your dream: your self-reflection on where you are right now and the degree to which you love your current results.

On a scale of 1 to 5, where 1 is "not satisfied" and 5 is "I love my health," how satisfied are you with your current health conditions? Assign a number on the scale and write it down. You can do this on a separate sheet of paper or fill in the appropriate bubble in the scale on page 77. Be honest and clear. Knowing where you are is the beginning of the road to the life you truly want.

Love and relationships

Now, write another header on a separate blank page: "Love and Relationships."

You might be a person who longs to have a beautiful, deep, fun, passionate relationship with a loving and caring partner. Maybe that hasn't been happening, but that is your longing, and you feel discontent because you don't yet have this. Perhaps you would love to deepen and expand and have more fun in your current relationship. Maybe you would just like some closer friends or healthier communication with your family. When you pause and reflect, you might see that you have let some of these relationships go on autopilot. Think about what you might like from your current relationships or friendships, whether that is more fun, depth, caring, intimacy, or liveliness. Your longing and discontent might not relate to a romantic relationship. You might have discord with one of your adult children, your parents, your friends, or your coworkers. Perhaps your relationships are harmonious, but you desire greater depth in them. Tune in to what isn't working as well as areas for growth. Notice any inner voices of opposition or disagreement that crop up; pay attention to the internal objections, reasons, or excuses, and just let them be for now.

Take some time to identify longing and discontent in your relationships. On a scale of 1 to 5, how satisfied are you with your current relationships? Here, 1 is "I'm not having the relationships that matter to me," and 5 is "my relationships are one of the richest, wealthiest, most wondrous areas of my whole life." Assign a number on the scale and jot it down.

Vocation

The next headline on your paper should be "Vocation."

Your vocation is what you do with your time and talent—whether you earn income doing it or not.

Think about how you feel about your vocation. Do you feel stuck in a job you don't like? Do you like your work but not the long hours? Do you look forward to going to work every day? You might have had great success in your career, but now you want to know how far you can go and how high you can fly. Or maybe it's time for a change. This is all about your time and talent. Perhaps you've always wanted to write a book or start a business, but it feels as though that dream is just hanging there. Maybe you've long wanted to start your own nonprofit or to work in a different industry. Or you want to earn more money doing what you love. There's nothing wrong with that, with whatever longings come up as you tune in and notice what you're noticing.

On a scale of 1 to 5, where 1 is "I'm trading my time for money. I check my soul at the door" and 5 is "I get immense satisfaction from my vocation," how satisfied are you with your vocation? Assign a number on the scale. Write it down.

Time and money freedom

The final part of the life quadrant to consider is "Time and Money Freedom."

Would you love more freedom? Review the last few years of your life: Has your income remained relatively the same or only slightly improved? Are you feeling discontented with your ability for financial freedom? Money freedom means being able to do what you really want and to contribute to the causes and organizations that matter most to you. A lack of time and money freedom means missing important moments with those closest to you and not doing what you've always wanted to do. Think about these freedoms—trips you have yet to take, the home (or homes) you'd love to live in, hobbies you've yet explored, people you want to spend more time with—and consider what might be missing.

On a scale of 1 to 5, how satisfied are you with your current time and money freedom? Write it down.

The four quadrants

Now, looking at the four numbers you have written down, notice how you feel. Invoke your relationship with meta-cognition and notice yourself noticing your longing and discontent. As you become aware of what's happening inside you, pay attention to the area you most want to transform right now. Circle the area or areas that have the lowest ratings.

	Not Satisfied				Very Satisfied
Health and Well-Being	◯1	◯2	◯3	◯4	◯5
Love and Relationships	◯1	◯2	◯3	◯4	◯5
Vocation	◯1	◯2	◯3	◯4	◯5
Time and Money Freedom	◯1	◯2	◯3	◯4	◯5

Now, ask yourself: "How long have I felt discontent in each of these areas?" Be honest. I know some people who have longed for the love of their life and wonder if it is time to give up. Others have wanted to improve their health for decades but don't find time to go to the gym and can't seem to get past yo-yo diets. Look at the numbers you have written down and notice how long you have been discontented in these areas. If you have acquiesced to the status quo, this exercise can help you move forward in the direction of your dreams.

FROM DISCONTENT TO DESERVING

Brave Thinking Tool: Notice your longing and discontent
Bringing your inner rumblings to the surface empowers you to recognize what you deeply desire.

Teaching points
- Listen to your still, small voice of inspired insight, which will always guide you to your highest good.

- Practice telling yourself, "Up until now..." to uncouple your future from the past.

Exercise
- Assess the four quadrants of your life—health and well-being, love and relationships, vocation, and time and money freedom—rating your degree of satisfaction in each.

4

A LIFE YOU
WOULD LOVE

---

*"There is no pity for a man who moans about
living in one town and does not move to another."*

THE TALMUD

_____

The Book of My Life

Has many blank pages left.

So... What would I love?

_____

FOR MANY YEARS I dreamed of having my own ministry, the kind built on spiritual and scientific principles that transform lives, the way my own life had been transformed by that wonderful chaplain who sat at my bedside the night before my kidney surgery. I envisioned a global ministry with a permanent home that served our congregation and the larger community.

My first church service, however, was conducted on a marionberry farm. And nobody showed up.

Haven, my husband, along with his two brothers, had coinherited the 133-acre property in Oregon. We had this romantic notion of farming the land for a year, the earth sustaining us, our simple toil bringing us closer to God. Haven and I had completed seminary. Our plan was to lease the land after one year, using the proceeds to launch our ministerial careers. But I could not wait. The property came with a fairly new farmhouse, and even though farming was a full-time job, I went in search of a podium. A nearby church offered me a one-hundred-year-old wobbly lectern that I promptly set up in our living room.

On Sunday mornings, I would deliver a sermon, often to an empty living room. At this point, we had three young children, John, Rich, and Jennifer. Every now and then, one of the kids would wander into the living room, searching for toys. I counted them as congregants. On holidays, adult family members stopped by, primarily to visit us and enjoy the ham and egg brunch I'd set out after services.

Living off the land proved challenging. All children of suburbia, we had never farmed before. The first year, we worked endless, back-breaking hours only to end the harvest $10,000 in the red. We assured ourselves that a second year of farming would provide us the income to clear up the debts accumulated from the first "failed" year. Then we could earn enough from farming to further our ministry, which remained as stunted as the crops. Even close friends kindly told us we were only "playing" at being ministers.

We persevered, putting every penny that came our way into farming, enduring a severe freeze, one downpour after another, and mounds of moldy fruit. We had nurtured our crop, lavished it with care, and hoped for a good harvest so that we might better serve God—how much more honorable can you get?—but our efforts left us stone-cold broke.

After five years, we ended our farming career, hocking the tractor, refinancing the farm, and leasing the property to pay off our bills. What next? My still, small voice told me to take our ministry on the road—for a year! "How can we do that?" I argued in my mind. "We barely have enough to live on." I should mention that, by this time, we had a fourth child, Mat, and two cats. And yet, the idea of taking our ministry on the road filled me with a new sense of aliveness.

When you are considering a dream, ask yourself, "What would I love?" For years, I'd been planting, tilling, and

BRAVE THINKING TOOL

Ask yourself, "What would I love?"

picking by rote, convinced that farming was the only means to support our ministry. I had not allowed myself to cocreate with the Infinite and imagine a more vibrant alternative.

"Take what you have and go," the voice repeated. Finally, I agreed.

We bought an old Checker cab that had been painted blue and decorated it with rainbows. Then we hitched that cab to a packed twenty-eight-foot used travel trailer. We took off with four children, two cats, a stack of books to help me homeschool our kids, $300 in our pocket, and a dream in our hearts. We spent fifteen adventurous months on the road speaking at more than one hundred churches, from California to Florida to Canada. What our transportation lacked in style, it made up for in heart. At least everyone could see us coming.

As we headed home to Oregon at the end of the trip, a massive hailstorm struck. Hailstones the size of golf balls permanently pockmarked our Checker cab. After filing an insurance claim, we received a check for $2,500.

The paperwork accompanying our check cited the cause of damage as "act of God."

Clearly this was a sign. Instead of fixing the dented car, we put that "act of God" money in a special bank account and started a church, this time in an Odd Fellows Hall. We called our church Living Enrichment Center. For our first week of services, pretty much everyone I knew came—that is, twenty-two people. Sometimes, our group was as small as eight, which included our four kids, my husband, me, and two friends. Granted this was not the prettiest place to gather, with its uncomfortable metal chairs that had seen better days. The stained linoleum floor curled up at the edges. I expected the ministry to grow rapidly, because I knew that what I was teaching changed lives.

The Odd Fellows held their gatherings on Saturday nights, so we negotiated to come in early Sunday morning and clean everything—the room, the kitchen, and the toilets—in lieu of paying twenty-five dollars a week in rent. Every Sunday, I woke up early, went in, cleaned the place, and then changed my clothes to become the minister. The Odd Fellows Hall held 150 people, and every Sunday, we would dutifully set up the folding chairs, but after five years, only forty or fifty people attended on a weekly basis. Even when we began serving cookies and coffee after the service, we had the same result.

By now, I had earned my master's degree in counseling psychology and was working many hours a week doing therapy for thirty dollars an hour. I had to find a way to pay my portion of the family bills so I could justify to myself continuing in what others thought was simply a pipe dream.

I told myself all kinds of stories about what was keeping potential parishioners away. "It's the metal chairs. Who wants to sit on an uncomfortable folding chair on a Sunday?" "People don't know about us because we can't afford to advertise. They don't even know we're here for them." I even went so far as to blame the linoleum.

You've examined your life while reading this book, and you've noticed how it feels to repeat the same results while you yearn for something greater. When you hear yourself, as I did, say, "This is happening because..." and the "because" is something outside yourself, pause for a moment. We can blame the economy or our upbringing, but that only distances us from our dream. The reality is that people building careers in the same economy have varying degrees of success. Children raised in the same family can turn out very differently. And I guarantee that congregants sitting in chairs or pews more uncomfortable than ours were packing halls like mine across town and beyond. The circumstances we choose to blame may influence our results, but they do not control them. Besides, I noticed the regulars attending our services did benefit; I could tell from the light in their eyes. I would not abandon my dream.

I began listening to cassette tapes put out by a minister named Jack Boland, a leader in the Unity movement who drew thousands of people to his services each week. His bold message about dreaming resonated with me. Learning that he was speaking at a conference in Chicago, I bought a plane ticket and attended the conference, determined to meet him. Given our limited finances at the time, buying that ticket was a brazen move on my part. But I knew this man knew something that I did not because he was having success that I only imagined.

After listening to Jack Boland speak, I stood in line, thanked him for his words, and practically begged him to have breakfast with me in the morning.

"I'm doing a three-day seminar," he said. "I can't have breakfast with you." Then he hesitated and said, "I'll give you thirty minutes. Meet me in the hotel cafe at seven tomorrow morning."

The following morning, Jack didn't mince words. "So, how can I help?" he asked.

"I want to do what you're doing. I'm doing a version of it, but a little tiny version." I told him about my dream to expand the ministry, to attract more people to my transformational teaching and training.

"I can help you with that, but it's going to cost you."

I was stuck in my set of circumstances, trying to conceive of how I could achieve my dream with the resources I already had. I pulled back and asked, "How much?"

Put "How" on Hold

Jack encouraged me to stop thinking about the "how" and focus instead on what I deeply desired, which was to build my congregation. He told me that he planned to mentor three people over the next year. He had already selected the first two, Les Brown and Wayne Dyer, who would go on to become internationally acclaimed inspirational thinkers and spiritual leaders. His third mentee could be me, if I was willing to step out of my comfort zone. Jack taught me that building a life you would love has nothing to do with cost. If we look to our current circumstances to achieve results, we produce nothing but the same results we have always had. He showed me how to shift my thinking from relying on the past to imagining an inconceivable future. Jack became not only my mentor but a dear friend.

Supported by Jack's mentorship, our ministry began to grow beyond what the Odd Fellows Hall could accommodate. Instead of worrying about my "how" to make my dream happen with limited resources, I began to imagine the church of my dreams fully manifested. This shift in thinking breathed new life into my sermons. As word about our ministry spread, we moved several times, eventually winding up in the most unlikely house of worship, a rented movie theater in a suburban shopping mall. Each Sunday, with the smell of stale popcorn wafting through the air, I stood on the stage and preached into the inky darkness. The theater was so dark that I could see only the front half of the congregation. For a long time, I worried my sermons were boring, as a few restless churchgoers visibly shifted in their seats. Apparently, they were simply attempting to remove wads of gum from the bottom of their pumps and loafers or to find a comfortable spot where the busted seat springs did not stab into their backsides. During communion, I used to joke, "Do you want that with butter?" But I wasn't complaining. Our congregation now numbered 2,500.

With so many enthusiastic parishioners, the time had come for us to create specific plans to locate and purchase a permanent church home. I asked our congregation members to fill out vision cards describing their dream for the church. Based on those cards, I wrote a collective vision. Our goal was to move in ten years, by the year 2001, Living Enrichment Center's twentieth anniversary.

That same year, Jack Boland visited Oregon to speak at an event that we had planned. He had cancer, I knew, but I had no idea how soon he would be gone.

"Would I love more time?" he said. "Yes. But I am still making the very most of the time I have. And I'm so happy with what I've done with the life I've had."

He wanted to know my plans for the church. I told him about our visioning process for a global ministry with a permanent home. I spoke of our church home as if it already existed, describing the acreage with gardens, fountains, and a stream. "We have statues representing all the world's religions," I told him, "an auditorium with natural light streaming in to delight all in attendance, and a kids' village where children learn about their Higher Power in a way that feels inviting and fun. We have a retreat center and kitchen that feeds four hundred people at a time."

We had $40,000 in a building fund. I told Jack that our goal was to make a down payment on some land that year, and in ten years' time move into what we estimated would be a $10 million permanent home.

Jack responded, "Why would you try to squeeze the Infinite into a ten-year plan? Wouldn't you love your building this year?"

"Yes, but we have $40,000, and this is a $10 million dream." I gazed at my mentor with a look that said, "Get real, Jack."

"Have I not taught you anything?" he asked.

Once again, I had to be reminded that at this stage of dream-building continually asking "how" becomes a roadblock. "Right now, Mary, do you believe that *I believe* you can have your own church home this year?"

I knew the great faith of Jack Boland, and I could see that he was serious.

"Yes," I said. "I believe *you* believe we could have our home this year."

Then Jack said something that shot me full of hope. "Then believe in *my* belief."

Intellectually I knew it would be a huge stretch to raise the money for bare land, let alone a whole facility. Yet in that moment, in the presence of a mentor and friend who absolutely believed in Infinite possibilities, a corner of my mind opened.

Jack taught me to stop squeezing the Infinite into a time-bound plan driven by Common-Hour Thinking. If I would love having a church home for the community— this year—I should focus on the vision, not on the seeming impossibility of the circumstances. I was transported back to that hospital bed when I had a terminal diagnosis. I had to believe it was possible. And when I couldn't muster the faith myself, I borrowed someone else's.

"Believe in my belief," Jack said, and then we gave each other a hug, and I left. After that breakfast, I was a changed woman. The Infinite always has resources beyond what I know. Always. I kept a corner of my mind open to the possibility that I could have that building that year. Six weeks later, my beloved mentor passed away, but not before he gave me a few pieces of parting advice and counsel.

Months later, we received an eviction notice from the movie theater. The building was being converted into a multiplex, and we had thirty days to get out. We negotiated a deal to rent the parking lot and put up a great big circus tent where we could hold services until we found a place to go.

About the same time we received the eviction notice, I reached the difficult decision to end my marriage. It had been twenty-seven years since two frightened teenagers had said their "I do's" and eleven years since we used the insurance money from a battered cab to start a church. Although the church eventually flourished, our marriage had not. Haven and I loved our children. We loved God and devoted our lives to serving. Yet, at the deepest level of our beings, something was missing. I dreamed of a spiritual partnership, a marriage in which two souls melded into one, but true compatibility eluded us. Our relationship had stagnated long ago, but neither of us had wanted to acknowledge it.

Ever since I was little, I had relied on my father's quiet strength and wisdom to see me through rough spots. One afternoon I poured my heart out. "Dad," I began, "I want you to know what's been going on with me. It's no secret that I haven't been happy in my marriage for a long time."

"Yes, I know." He waited for me to continue.

"I know it's my decision, but I want to know what you think."

My dad leaned forward slowly, put his arm around me, and said what he always had when I found myself at a crossroads: "There is only one thing you *can* do. You do what gives you life."

Do what gives you life. I wept with relief.

An invitation from the Infinite

The two evictions—one from my marriage and one from our church home—happened almost simultaneously. Haven and I could no more squeeze into the narrow confines of our marriage than our growing church could stay in a movie theater that was being divided into three screens. After more than two and a half decades of marriage, Haven and I divorced. To this day, we remain close friends and celebrate our children's and grandchildren's milestones together.

Have you received an eviction notice in your own life? Whatever the circumstance, that notice is an invitation from the Infinite into a greater experience.

It did not take ten years to realize our 100,000-square-foot building with the sanctuary, the kitchen, and the children's village. It took ten months. We found a property in Wilsonville, Oregon, just south of Portland. A rehabilitation center built by the state, the 100,000-square-foot facility had long been abandoned. Many rodents, however, had moved in. The price was $3 million, which was less than what we had planned to pay for bare land. Our congregation came together to loan the church funds that allowed us to move in that year and then to clean up the space to make it beautiful.

I have seen so many things happen over the years when people apply Brave Thinking—this proven, reliable, repeatable system of transformation—to their lives. We truly can accomplish far more than we think is possible when we refuse to limit our thinking to what seems possible. Eventually, Living Enrichment was serving four thousand people a week. And we launched an international ministry, reaching more than one hundred countries through weekly shortwave radio broadcasts out of the Radio for Peace International in Costa Rica, where we would send my weekly messages. I thought this dream come true would last forever.

A bold question

This Brave Thinking Tool—Ask yourself, "What would I love?"—is a bold question that opens you to a power that will reveal itself to you in profound ways. You don't need to ask other people what to do. You don't need to consult an expert or a guru or a therapist. You just need to ask yourself.

A dream isn't something you can outsource; it comes from within. Asking yourself, "What would I love?" is a form of spiritual decision-making, because you've gone to the highest source for guidance.

Most of us think that we don't have the life we love because we don't have sufficient resources: money, time, training, or talent. Logically, a converted cab, crammed travel trailer, and $300 was grossly insufficient to launch a mobile ministry for more than a year. And yet that pivotal experience set me on a path to fulfill my dream. We think that if we have certain assets, everything will be easier, but that's not true. I promise you that none of those things makes a dream become a reality. There is never a money problem or a time problem when it comes to dream-building. It is always an awareness problem. The truth—that we already possess precisely what we need to achieve our dreams—is something we often overlook. As you acquire greater awareness, you will transform your results, starting with the resources you already have.

Of course, this is easier said than done. Many of us believe so strongly in our problems, assuming they are insurmountable obstacles. But this kind of thinking can be changed with an expansion of your awareness, the most important part of yourself to develop.

Consider the two aspects of your nature: you are a spiritual being having a human experience. That is, you have a spiritual nature and a human nature. Both aspects make up who and what you are. The spiritual side of your nature is ever moving upward, pressing you to become more of who you are capable of being. This part of you propels you forward and upward, wanting you to fulfill your dreams. Your human nature looks to existing situations and conditions to determine what is possible. Now that you have learned to notice what you are noticing, you can notice which side of your nature you listen to most, and, if need be, shift the focus.

As your awareness evolves, your circumstances change. Circumstances cannot stay the same when understood and perceived through greater awareness. Your current results stem from your thinking and awareness. Even if you see your circumstances as hopeless, you can learn how to perceive something greater that existed all along, the patterns that you missed noticing earlier. This is Brave Thinking in action. Once you understand and embrace the invisible yet immutable spiritual laws, you can produce incredible results. You have everything you need to live a life you would love. You are connected to an Infinite source of energy that resonates, but most of us fail to understand how to tap into such a power.

Einstein said, "No problem can be solved from the same level of consciousness that created it."

Right now, there is a gap between your current life and the life you want, and what you do in this "gap" space is crucial.

I often hear people complain that they don't have enough time to do what they truly want. But every one of us gets the same amount of time each day. Nobody gets more than twenty-four hours, and nobody gets less. If you feel as though you don't have enough time, consider that it is not an issue of time but of your relationship with time. Right now, there is a gap between your current life and the life you want, and what you do in this "gap" space is crucial.

In the absence of knowing how to navigate that gap, you will likely collapse into the familiar—your old life—because it feels safe. You know exactly what happens if you keep living that life: more of the same. Oddly enough, such familiarity feels good. It is "normal," not bad, to drift back into your old ways, even if they were not life-giving.

This gap is something I know well, having come up against it many times. On the eve of my kidney surgery, the chaplain helped me to envision a life better than the one I had. There was no "how" involved. When I imagined myself becoming a teacher, I wasn't thinking about how I could afford a university education and attain a four-year degree. When I imagined walking my little boy to his kindergarten classroom, I wasn't thinking about who would babysit him after school. The "how" was left out, the "what" crystal clear. This is a process we can master: imagining the impossible, then increasing our awareness so we can create it.

Being specific about your dream allows you to see a picture of the life you would love, one you can literally and energetically step inside. In the book of Genesis (which means "the beginning of all creation"), we learn that everything originates from thought. In the beginning there was the void. Space. Nothingness. God had a very specific purpose—to fill the emptiness. But God did not begin, "Let there be... whatever." God said, "Let there be light." God specified light, and light came into being. The same is true for your dream: start with what you want, and then envision it having already happened.

The Infinite has a language. It has a way to commune and communicate with us, and it is as precise as mathematics. X always equals X; it will never be anything different. The quality of your life is directly related to the quality of questions you are willing to ask and the vibration you think from.

Think bigger, bolder, and *braver*.

Dream of what you would absolutely love,

not asking *how* but only *what*.

What led me on my unlikely journey of failed farming, road preacher, and minister/janitor at the Odd Fellows Hall was that, early on, I boldly answered the question "What would I love?" And I am confident that responding to this question will be the bedrock of the journey you are undertaking right now. As humans, we are trained to ask "why" or "how" questions, but rarely "what" questions, at least when it comes to imagining our future. Why and how questions direct you back to an old filing system in your brain that spits out familiar answers. Partnering with the Infinite is an invitation to move beyond what you have done before or even what you think is possible. Using the Brave Thinking Tool from chapter 2, Notice what you are noticing, you will pay more attention to the questions you are asking. Then, tell that part of you wondering how, "I'll talk to you later. Right now, I'm focusing on what that I would love."

When this part starts chattering—and it does when you start pursuing a life you would love—it might say, "How are you going to do that? Where's the money going to come from? How will you find the time?" That limiting part of you argues for the status quo, but—as of right now—your dream is beyond the status quo. You want to go forward now, and that contracted part is arguing for why you can't. That's normal. But you don't have to keep indulging those doubts. To paraphrase an old parable often attributed to the Cherokee, in each of us there are two wolves. One is good, full of compassion and love—this is the source of life and expansion in all of us. But we each have another wolf: the voices of jealousy and fear and self-doubt that we have accumulated from Common-Hour Thinking. These two wolves are constantly fighting each other, waging a war inside us. So, which one wins? The one we feed.

The part of you that wants to go forward has the power to triumph over the part of you that argues for why you must stay put. If you let that old part win, you'll keep living the same life. Instead, keep increasing your awareness, paying attention to your thoughts, feeding those that are expansive and turning away from contractive ones. Starve that part of you that wants to know how or when, and feed the part of you that stays connected to your dream.

To channel your inner dream builder, you need to be specific, imagining a reality beyond what you can create with the resources you have right now. Go to the Infinite, asking for guidance and being receptive to the messages you receive. Think bigger, bolder, and *braver*. Dream of what you would absolutely love, not asking *how* but only *what*.

Then you can tune in to the right frequency, getting as specific as possible and imagining the dream as if it has already been realized.

After all, Martin Luther King Jr.'s oral masterpiece was not the "I Have a Plan" speech. It was his "I Have a Dream" speech that will resonate throughout history. Dr. King stood for a dream before he knew how to bring it about. He was willing to do the work of aligning himself with that vision, to let the desire and inspiration win over the part of him that doubted his ability. That same power resides in you.

Everyone can dream

At one of my seminars, a woman named Anna raised her hand and asked, "But, Mary, you don't understand, I *can't* dream." She was upset, angry even, with the implication that all you need to do is think bravely and act in harmony with your vision, starting with the "what." Maybe you've had similar thoughts, such as "it's easier for other people" or "my struggles are real!"

I could tell that Anna was having a hard time, so I brought her up on the stage and asked her to sit down. Then I put my arm around her. She began by saying, "I can't dream because..."

I interrupted her. "I'm sure there are reasons that led you to believe you can't dream, but wait for a moment. If you keep breathing, you are going to have a life three years from now. That version of life will be by design, or by default."

I invited her to talk about her life three years in the future. Since results in her life were inevitable, wouldn't she love great health? Yes, she said she would, adding that she wanted her husband to enjoy great health, as well. I asked where she wanted to be living three years from now. She replied that she and her husband had always wanted to live in New Mexico in a house built before the 1940s with an adobe arch doorway. But she had convinced herself that could never happen.

I said, "Let's try this. Imagine you and your husband have great health. You're living in Santa Fe in an adobe house built before the 1940s. You love your new home."

She sat up straighter and already looked more energetic and liberated.

I asked if she'd traveled much or had a place she would love to visit. I've worked with people all over the world, and they always want to travel to a place unlike home. People from Paris rarely dream of visiting the Eiffel Tower, for example. Anna's response surprised me. With tears in her eyes, she said, "I've always wanted to go to Wyoming."

Wyoming is a wonderful state, but in my experience, people who dream of travel tend to envision themselves visiting the Taj Mahal, watching the sunset in Santorini, climbing Machu Picchu, and so on. But my job is not to judge or negotiate with somebody else's dream. What I immediately noticed, however, was the way Anna lit up when she said, "Wyoming."

"Tell me more," I urged.

"I've wanted to go there for years and volunteer for two weeks," she said. "There's a place in Wyoming where you can volunteer and love back to life these animals that have been used in medical experiments. I want to do that."

What a beautiful vision for someone who only moments before told me she could not dream. Many of us are like this. We say we do not have a dream, or cannot dream, when we are afraid. This woman could dream; but she didn't have support, someone to encourage her in imagining a future better than her present. When you are stuck in your own thinking and don't have the support to choose from a different place inside yourself, you are likely to keep living the same life.

That's why reading this book gives you a huge advantage. Together we are going to put support structures in your life with the Brave Thinking Tools so that you can liberate yourself from the constrictions that lead to your repeatedly realizing the same results. If you keep breathing, you are going to have a life three years from now. That is a guarantee. As your awareness increases, that life will be a richer, fuller one, a life you truly love.

EXERCISE: Create a Full-Spectrum Vision Statement

A vision statement is an important part of blueprinting. Remember that everything is created twice, first in the mind and then in form. An idea has a frequency to it and becomes a pattern, and that pattern evolves into something that we can touch, see, smell, taste, feel, or experience. We begin with ideas that become the blueprint for our dream. We "transmit" energy in a few ways—through our thoughts (measurable units of energy); the images that flash upon the screen of our mind when we think of something specific; and the feelings we experience, which amplify our energy. This energy has a generative and creative influence on our experience of reality. The vision statement is a blueprint of the dream you are building—first in energetic form and then in physical form.

The vision statement is a blueprint of the dream you are building—first in energetic form and then in physical form.

In its first iteration, your vision statement may contain just a few sentences in each quadrant—health and well-being, love and relationships, vocation, and time and money freedom. As you spend more time with your vision and connect emotionally with the life you desire, your statement will expand. Fully fleshed out vision statements typically fill two to three pages. Keep updating your statement as you move through the dream-building process.

To build a dream successfully, you need to know what you'd love in your health and well-being, your love and relationships, your vocation, and your time and money freedom. Revisit your Life Assessment exercise from chapter 3, reviewing how you graded your satisfaction level for each of these quadrants. Likely, you identified one or two areas of greatest longing, where you desire significant changes in your life; however, you will still want to address all four quadrants in your vision statement to lay a foundation for full-spectrum success. Grab a new piece of paper and write at the top: "My vision for a life I would love living..." This is going to be your life, so it needs to be accurate and passionate. This is not the time to hold back. Dream full-out!

Start by listing what you would love in each quadrant. Next you create a vivid mental representation of the life that results from having, being, and doing everything on that list.

For example, in his health quadrant, one man I worked with, Andrew, wrote, "I am so grateful to wake up each morning and bounce out of bed, eager to start the day, especially the days I babysit my grandson. I have the stamina to spend hours playing dinosaur, chasing this energetic three-year-old as he roars with glee." When Andrew composed his vision statement, he had a nerve injury and could barely walk. Notice that he did not write that he desired to be pain free. Your subconscious mind has no filter and no sense of humor. It reads the word "pain," which has a negative vibration. Describe your vision for optimal health, not what you seek to banish.

Here are a few elements to keep in mind while composing your vision statement:

1   Write in the present tense, as if your dream has already manifested. You want to direct your vision to the present moment.

2   Express gratitude. How has living your dream caused you to become more thankful and appreciative in various areas of your life?

3   Use words that evoke emotion for you.

4   Remember to put the "how" on hold. At this point in the dream-building process, the question is "*What* would I love?"

5   Be as specific as possible. Remember, the mind thinks in pictures. If your vision is for a dream home, imagine

yourself in that space, just as I imagined the feeling of my son's hand when I was walking him to his first day of kindergarten.

Health and well-being

Let's start with health and well-being. Review the results of your health and well-being assessment. You wrote a number from 1 to 5. If it is not a 5, what would move it up the scale? Imagine yourself standing in the same place you are now, but three years later, describing your optimal health. Write the words, "I am so happy and grateful now that..." and then complete the sentence with what you would love. People who have done this exercise have written things such as "I sleep well, I wake rested"; "I have stamina, strength, and aliveness"; "I love biking three times a week." The more precise your description, the more closely your brain can begin to replicate the result you envision.

Love and relationships

Now, do the same with your relationships. What in your relationships would be happening that would answer your longing and discontent? What's happening for you in that area when you have exactly what it is you love? Is it a family with a specific number of children? A new friendship? Finding your soulmate? Perhaps you have healed an old rift with someone once close to you.

What would you love? Write it down: "I'm so happy and grateful now that..." and let the Infinite know what you would like, specifically: "I have met the love of my life. We are walking on the beach planning our future. We are holding hands. I love the safe feeling I have with this person." Design your dream. Speak from it. Imagine the dream as if it has already happened.

One client, Lorri Hart, thought long and hard about the qualities she sought in a soulmate, writing that she desired "a man of integrity." In crafting her ignited vision statement, she also drew images of the Eiffel Tower as she visualized a life of romance and love. Lorri wound up meeting her dream man, who took her to Paris and proposed on top of the Eiffel Tower.

Vocation

Let's turn to your vocation now. You might know what you want to do but feel unsure about how to turn it into a business or a career. Describe your ideal day. What are you doing? Who are you with? Write, "I'm so happy and grateful now that..." Now build your dream. Why not imagine people you love working with who are creative and energetic? If you are highly professional, smart, and deeply committed to your ideal job, dream up that job. If you would love to own your own business, describe what makes that business successful. It is three years from now: what is happening in your vocation that you love?

Time and money freedom

The last quadrant to work with is time and money freedom, which includes philanthropy. What would you do with more time and money freedom? Would you spend more time with your children or grandchildren, attending their soccer and basketball games? Would you travel? If so, where specifically would you visit? If you would love to be a world traveler, name the places you go. Simply writing "I want to travel the world" doesn't cut it. If you envision yourself as a philanthropist, are you doing it to make a difference in a corner of the world that matters most to you?

Getting started

Having trouble getting started? Some people break the ice with what they don't want and then write their vision of the opposite. Others find the vision by listing their responses to the prompt "this is what I want for certain..."

As you ask "what would I love in my health and well-being, love and relationships, vocation, and time and money freedom?" you are creating a blueprint for a life you would love. Learn to work with Spirit and energy, which may sound esoteric or even "woo-woo," but this is a practical and scientific process. Think of it this way: imagine using an old television set. If you wanted to watch a specific program, you had to turn to a particular channel, which is another way of saying you had to be on the right frequency. In the case of an old radio, too, you had to turn the dial just so to land on the right frequency for the station you wanted—otherwise, you got static. Even search engines work this way: if your search terms aren't clear, the results can be confusing or overwhelming. To find the right channel for your dream, be specific. The Infinite is sensitive and responsive to your focus, so the clearer you express what you want, the easier it will be for you to have it. To work with what is called "the law of specificity," you need clarity. Images are required.

Remember my vision when I was in that hospital bed, imagining the scene in which I dropped off my son on his first day of kindergarten? It was a moving picture, like a movie, and I was inside it. I was not trying to move toward that life. I stepped into it and was imaginably living that life. The experience was visceral. I could feel it. I was *having* that life. Likewise, start with a vivid image of what you want to create, and then envision it having already happened.

Designing a clear picture is easier than you might think. Close your eyes and visualize your current home. Think of your front door and really *see* that door. Now go inside, imagine your kitchen sink. Now go to your bedroom and imagine your bed.

Notice that you did not see the individual letters as D-O-O-R, S-I-N-K, and B-E-D. You saw a picture of the door, the sink, and the bed. Words are not enough. Goals and affirmations can only get us so far, and until we envision what our dream looks like and feels like, we are writing our dreams in the sand.

Designing a picture of the life you would love to live involves this same visual practice. If your pictures are too vague—"I just want a better house"—the Infinite cannot cash that check. Be specific. The universe does not hold back its abundance from any of us, but we dictate how much of it we enjoy by our most dominant vibration. If you have a pattern of struggle regarding money, you will continue to establish struggle in that area until you change your major operating frequency.

As well as creating vivid pictures of the life you would love, you need to create an emotional connection to that life. Emotions such as gratitude and joy amplify and transmit your vision in the energy of the Infinite and so are vital to your success. When I used this practice in that hospital bed, I held my little boy's hand in my mind's eye. He was five years old. I realized that if I could feel the warmth of his hand, I must be alive in that future that meant so much to me. Thinking that thought, and seeing it in my mind, transformed the frequency I was living in, from one of self-loathing and toxicity to one that ultimately saved my life.

Test Your Dream with Five Essential Questions

You now have the beginnings of a new life, either a vision in your mind or one committed to paper. You may think that testing this dream is the opposite of what you should do at this point, that you should trust the life you've envisioned and go after it. But you want to be sure that this is what you would absolutely love. When something as important as your life is at stake, you want to be confident that you have chosen to pursue the dream closest to your heart. You can learn to separate your true desires from your passing fancies, those things that diminish over time. If you have children, you know what I mean. Little ones may plead for the latest overpriced toy they insist all their friends have. Even though it goes against your better judgment, you finally relent and buy it. A week later you find the former object of your child's desire broken and buried at the bottom of the toy chest, never to be played with again. As adults, we like to think of ourselves as being less fickle, yet we frequently pursue dreams that lack substance and wind up casually discarded. How do you know you have chosen a dream that will bring the fulfillment you truly want? How can you know your dream is right for you?

We are going to subject your dream to some rigorous tests, but these tests differ vastly from those you've undergone before. Whatever dream you decide to build, you will be putting your time, talent, and effort into it. You will literally be trading your life for it—your one precious life—so you want to be sure it is something you would love. That's why we test the dream. If your dream became your life three years from now—with the health and well-being, love and relationships, vocation, and time and money freedom results—would you love it? This is key. If you would not love it, then the dream is neither strong enough nor big enough. Anything less than love will not supply the energy needed to see you through the process.

Notice where your dream is right now in your mind. For most of us, it is a life we have only imagined, somewhere *out there*, which is a good place to start. But to continue, we must act decisively in the direction of our dream to see it come alive.

Many people wonder, at this point, "Am I worthy of this dream?" But the truth is you should be asking the opposite: "Is this dream worthy of me?" There are five questions to ask yourself and answer honestly, with heart. Every time a new idea comes to you that feels expansive and you can imagine yourself loving, make sure it passes these five points.

Question #1: Does imagining my dream give me life?

This is your starting point. Feel your own energy regarding the dream. Does the mere thought of your dream quicken your pulse? Do you feel an amplified sense of aliveness as you vividly imagine living the fulfillment of this dream? Trust that. Your soul will never lie to you. As an ordained minister without a congregation, I dreamed of taking my ministry on the road for a year with my family. That dream reinvigorated my sense of aliveness. Don't mistake your dream for a "should" or a promise to someone else. If your dream is just a big "I should," then you won't harness the energy to bring your desire into form. Ask yourself: Does it give *me* life?

Question #2: Does this dream align with my core values?

You cannot pursue a dream that forces you to compromise your fundamental sense of integrity. In this spiritual venture of dream-building, you must remain true to yourself at each crossroads. Will pursuing your dream cause you to sacrifice your family? Will it put your health at risk? A true dream will never ask you to sacrifice a core value. Many of us have never explored or identified our core values. Take a moment and consider your deathbed. What will you regret? At the end of your life, what will have mattered most to you?

Question #3: Will creating this dream cause me to grow?

Take the life you have now and hold it up against the life you would love. Would getting there require you to grow? Sometimes we mistake a worthy goal for our dream, but your dream will cause you to expand. You will be grateful for the person you are required to become to achieve your dream.

Question #4: Does my dream require help from a Higher Power?

If you know exactly how to bring about what you would love, then that's a goal, not a dream. If you don't know how to make your dream happen, then you need help from a Higher Power—what I call the Infinite. Whatever name you use, the point is the same: you don't have to do this alone. In fact, you can't do it on your own. You cannot even take one breath on your own. Were it not for the Spirit animating you right now, your body would collapse to the floor. When you call on a power higher than yourself, you reach a higher level of connection with the Infinite Intelligence that knows all things and brings about not only your dream, but the person you become in the process.

Question #5: Will creating this dream bring good for others?

One of the questions people ask is, "My dream is finding the love of my life. How is that dream good for anyone other than just me?" You might be challenged to wonder if there is any good in this for others. Certainly, the dream bene-fits your partner. Also, notice how when you are out in the world, say, at the grocery store, and happen upon two peo-ple who are clearly in love. Can you not feel that love? Are you not blessed by that? When you see others achieve their dreams, you can feel blessed at some level, too. As you open yourself to greater possibilities, you can easily see the good that can bless others just by living the life you love.

EXERCISE: Time Machine (Stepping Into a New Reality)

Time Machine is an exercise we use in my seminars, and with it, you can apply all the tools you have learned so far to visualize the life you would love. Note that Time Machine is only useful if you have a coherent dream, exactly what you want your life to look like. I'm going to take you through the exercise right now and, ideally, you will practice this activ-ity many times with a close friend or family member who will ask you questions and guide you through the process. Here's how it works.

First, I invite you to stand up, if you feel so inclined, so you can access more of your energy. You don't have to stand, but doing so can help. Now, you are reading this book, so let's start there.

Based on what you've learned thus far in this book, consider what you want your life to look like three years from today. Using the information from your vision statement, think again about all four key areas of your life. Now imagine it is three years from now. You're catching up with a dear friend you haven't spoken with in all that time. And your friend says, "Tell me what's new and exciting in your life." That's your moment for stepping into the time machine.

So, here we go. I am going to invite you to join me in the future.

Imagine you have a time machine. The time machine is safe, reliable, and has the power to transport you to the future. Can you see this machine in front of you? Try to imagine what it would look like. Perhaps it resembles something from your favorite sci-fi movie or a Disneyland ride.

Now, get in the time machine. In a moment, you are going to meet me three years in the future, and I will be ready to hear what you achieved. You relentlessly pursued your dream and accomplished the impossible. Unlike a "traditional" time machine, where you have no idea what has transpired from present day to the future, when you step out of *this* time machine you will be three years older, and you will have full knowledge of each moment that you lived for the last three years. This means you will be prepared to tell me about what your life is *now*... in other words, in what was the future *before* you got into your time machine. You won't say, "I *will* do this." You will say, "I have done this!" Now, let's leave the current year and travel into the future. Imagine yourself landing three years from now. You step out of the time machine and there I am. Let's have our conversation.

"Oh my gosh," I say, "I am so happy to see you! Tell me about your life..."

You may begin with, "Oh, Mary, I love my life! Let me tell you about my life."

You then share your health and well-being results, your love and relationships results, your vocation results, as well as your time and money freedom results. How do you feel to have done so much in a relatively short amount of time? In this life (albeit imagined), what you dreamed is now your reality.

"Wow, that's incredible," I say. "You have an amazing life. I am so happy for you, deep in my heart. I can see that life, and it looks *so* good on you. Take your right hand, put it on your left shoulder, and your left hand and put it on your right. Say, 'Good job. Way to listen.'"

Time Machine is a powerful exercise. Think of it as a technology that puts you on the frequency that is a match for your dream to come true. Like any exercise, the more you do it, the stronger you become, able to hold that frequency throughout your day and ultimately achieve your desired results. You will feel increasingly confident and comfortable talking about the future as if it has already happened. This is important, because, as Einstein explained, "the distinction made between past, present, and future is nothing more than a persistent, stubborn illusion." The leading theoretical physicists of our age, Einstein, Feynman, and Hawking, agreed that the past, present, and future exist together within a four-dimensional universe, where the fourth dimension is time. What's more, in his final paper, Stephen Hawking wrestled with the concept of the multiverse, where many parallel realities exist simultaneously. So when you use your imagination to inhabit the future, you are calling a potential reality into the present. This is how we manifest new realities, how we create unlikely futures.

This process will also embed dreams deeply in your subconscious. As a living vibration, the neurons in your brain will begin to associate these ideas and accomplishments with you, causing them to "fire and wire" together. As you use your imagination to "time travel" into the future, you build new synaptic connections. This isn't hocus-pocus. It is real science. This resonance with a desired future can become your go-to highway for information, seeing the future as if it has already happened, allowing you to establish a relationship with your dream. The more you interact with it, the stronger your dream life will become, and the easier it will be to build.

A LIFE YOU WOULD LOVE

Brave Thinking Tool: Ask yourself, "What would I love?"
Without limits or conditions, choose the best life imaginable.

Teaching points

- Put the "how" on hold and focus instead on "what" the dream is that you deeply desire.

- Test your dream with five essential questions: (1) Does imagining my dream give me life? (2) Does this dream align with my core values? (3) Will creating this dream cause me to grow? (4) Does my dream require help from a Higher Power? (5) Will creating this dream bring good for others?

Exercises

- Create a full-spectrum vision statement—a blueprint of the dream you are building, first in energetic form and then in physical form.

- Step into a new reality with the Time Machine, a technology that will whisk you three years into a future where you are already living your dream.

PART II

BRIDGING

BUILDING A LIFE you would love takes more than knowing what you want. It requires creating a welcoming environment for your dream to grow. Many people get excited about their vision but struggle to maintain the momentum to move their dream forward, and so sink back into their old life. When it comes to dreaming, most people stop right there: with the dream. But that's only phase one in this process of dream-building. You want more than a great blueprint, after all; you want a great life. *Before building your dream, you need to systematically expand your thinking to bridge the gap between what you truly desire and what you believe is possible.*

In "Blueprinting," you created a vivid mental image of the life you would love. In "Bridging," you will learn to tame your fears and focus your attention and energy on becoming that person in the picture. This next section is about using science- and technology-based principles to hone your thinking.

Think again about tuning your brain like a radio to a station, a frequency of vibration that raises your thinking from the mundane to the extraordinary. Instead of automatically tuning in to your old standby "95.5 FM Common-Hour Classics" that plays nonstop negative input, you consciously select a channel that supports your dream. Such a channel will both *receive* from a Higher Source and *transmit* through your brain the thoughts that will transform you and the world around you. Frustrating life circumstances can shift quickly and easily when you attack them from a higher frequency. Tuned to this frequency, you befriend fear instead of being paralyzed by it. You will deepen your commitment to the dream, refusing to be distracted; let go of old paradigms; and discover how to turn any failure into a stepping stone. Bridging is all about matching your thinking to the life you would love.

5

COMMON-HOUR THINKING VERSUS BRAVE THINKING

"So many of us choose our path out of fear disguised as practicality. What we really want seems impossibly out of reach and ridiculous to expect so we never dare to ask the universe for it. I'm saying that you can ask the universe for it... letting the universe know what you want and working toward it, while letting go of how it comes to pass."

JIM CARREY

Common-Hour Thinking

Tricks us into believing

Things that just aren't true.

FEAR OF FAILURE and fear of rejection are two of the biggest barriers to our dreams. We never rid ourselves of fear. It is an automatic reaction that alerts us to physical or emotional danger, both real and imagined. (A loud noise in the middle of the night jolts you awake, setting off your internal alarm. Someone has broken into the house. Call 911. Or maybe the icemaker is on the fritz again.) Fear also plays an important role in dream-building. Without fear, there would be no need for Brave Thinking.

Fear shows up uninvited, often triggering a fight-or-flight response. Common-Hour Thinking directs us to flee, as if we were facing a tiger. Our modern-day techniques for "running away" from scary thoughts include numbing and distraction. Some people turn to alcohol or drugs to avoid thoughts like "I'll never amount to anything," "now everyone will know how flawed I really am," or "I can't face failing *again*." Others escape by binge-watching the newest high-tension drama series on Netflix. But when the screen fades to black after the final episode, the fearful thought returns. Fear of loneliness, fear of getting old, fear of failure—even the most successful people encounter every one of these.

Brave Thinkers, however, recognize and acknowledge fear instead of hiding from it under the covers. In fact, for them, fear is a wake-up call. When fear presents itself, you have an opportunity to observe what happens to your mind and body from a more objective perspective. Where in your body do you first sense fear? What is your mind telling you? By accepting fear, you do not have to live fearfully. Brave Thinkers acknowledge fear as integral to dream-building. They notice what they're experiencing, such as a raised heart rate, shallow breathing, or tightened gut, and use that adrenaline rush to boldly ask themselves, "What would I love?"

Our thoughts travel as electrical and chemical signals through the billions of neurons in our brain. Having repeated thoughts at high levels of concentration releases neuro-transmitters at elevated rates that stimulate the growth of new connections between the neurons in a particular path-way. If you practice Brave Thinking—that is, if you focus on living your dream as a reality—you wire your brain for manifesting that dream. By contrast, if you rely on Common-Hour Thinking to address difficulty—looking to your circumstance to tell you what's possible—you think fearful thoughts. Your brain becomes wired to fear and scarcity, leaving no room for the dream to grow.

Early in my first marriage, my go-to response was fear. Whenever difficulty arose—which it did, often—I panicked, imagining the worst-case scenario. Were it not for an inci-dent that taught me a valuable technique to tame fear, we might never have built the church.

Once my two little boys were old enough for preschool, I began pursuing my undergraduate teaching degree. By that time, I was deeply unhappy in my marriage. Wed as teenagers, my husband and I lacked the skill set to navigate serious conflict. I was raised in a happy environment. My parents never fought. My husband grew up in a highly volatile family. So we had disparate modeling for solving conflict. One thing we both agreed on, however, was that the *other* person was the problem. I wanted a divorce, but we had two children and couldn't afford to live separately.

While reading the university newspaper one day, I saw an ad looking for couples to participate in an eight-week encounter group exploring techniques for better communication. Both Haven and I thought this was a great idea.

The first evening, eight couples met with counselors from Portland State University and Julia, a grandmotherly woman who headed the psychiatry department at what is now called Oregon Health & Science University. When they asked for volunteers to share their stories, my hand shot up. My husband winced, with a look on his face that said, "She's going to make it all about me." I told my story, and it *was* all about him, ending with "So that's why I'm getting a divorce."

Julia then asked Haven if he had been listening. "Of course," he said. "But there are a few things I'd like to say—"

She cut him off. "If you've been listening, you'll be able to repeat what Mary just said." She explained the difference between authentic listening and merely waiting for your turn to talk. "If you've been preparing your comeback, how could you hear your wife's concerns?"

By this point, I was thoroughly puffed up. The psychiatrist was on *my* side. She understood what I had to put up with each day. But then she turned that sweet grandmotherly gaze on me.

"Mary, because of your hurt, you're telling your husband you don't love him. How long are you going to punish him? One day? The rest of your life? How long?"

The first step in learning to communicate during conflict, she explained, is to let the other person talk, then follow up with, "This is what I heard you say." You are not implying agreement, but rather acknowledging what your partner has expressed.

She asked me to invest in the marriage for six more months. I was a tough case. I agreed to thirty days.

Haven and I took away valuable tools from that first session. We pledged to listen to and acknowledge one another and to participate in whatever the other person felt was important. A week later, my husband came home excited about an upcoming lecture he'd heard about on innovative thinking. The lecture sounded like a good opportunity to support my husband's interests.

I don't recall the speaker's name, but I will never forget what he told us. "The next time something happens, and you're tempted to immediately say, 'This is bad,' hit your internal pause button and wait three days. Turn up the volume on your curiosity and look for the good. See if you can find some possible good in a situation that you regard as a total negative." The idea that I didn't have to suffer or wait for circumstances to change to be happy constituted a major shift for me. In the past, I'd assumed that whatever was happening determined the quality of my life.

Two days after the lecture, my husband came home from work, his face ashen. He'd been laid off from his job as a milkman, along with many of his fellow workers. Fear rose in my throat. We had children to support; I was in school.

Pause and look for any possible good

On the verge of panic, I remembered what the speaker had said: "Hit your internal pause button. Wait three days and look for the good." We grabbed a piece of paper to write down the possible good in this situation: Haven no longer had a ninety-minute commute to and from work. Perhaps he could find a job closer to home. He could pursue a higher-paying position. Maybe he wouldn't have to work such long hours. Creating this list calmed us and gave me a sense of empowerment. No matter how bad things appeared, I was not helpless. I had access to power that could bring positive changes to our lives.

Until that time, I'd been more of a "Negative Nellie," someone easily devastated by bad news. Like many people, my mind would become consumed by the problem at hand. Of course, whatever we focus on expands. The larger the problem loomed in my mind, the more fearful I'd become. Granted, nobody enjoys losing a job, especially when it represents a family's sole income. In the past, this news would have sent me into full panic mode, paralyzed by the ramifications of a dire future that had yet to happen. I'd be thinking, "I'll have to quit school. We won't be able to pay the rent." But now, for the first time, I didn't let this seemingly bad news overtake my life. My husband's unexpected unemployment did not devastate me. I did not have to wait for the problem to be fixed to enjoy life again.

In less than a week, Haven found a new position. He was still a milkman, but the job was closer to home, required fewer hours, and paid a higher wage. Just like that, something seemingly terrible had been turned around by pausing and seeking the good. The same thing happened in our marriage. I paused, looked for the good, and we stayed together. That thirty days I'd promised the grandmotherly psychiatrist turned into twenty more years. Haven started seminary and I followed two years later. We built a congregation together and we raised four children together, all because we found the good in the so-called bad.

You can change your relationship with fear. The next time something seemingly bad happens, instead of panicking, hit your internal pause button and look for any possible good. Open your calendar and schedule your upset for three days later. Most of the time, you won't have to keep the appointment.

Consider a scenario that has caused many a budding entrepreneur to panic: a lawsuit. Imagine your business gets slapped with a $1 million lawsuit. But your business is not even worth $1 million. If your first thought is "this will end me; I'm ruined," no one will blame you. But my friend and colleague Bill Harris took a different approach. A lifelong student of ancient and modern research into the nature of the mind, in 1989 Bill founded the Centerpointe Research Institute, an organization dedicated to helping people achieve personal growth through the power of meditation. He developed a ground-breaking audio technology that incorporates subtle sound underneath and inside of music that induces deep, healing states of meditation.

Bill found investors, and the company began to grow. Then one day, a subpoena arrived, informing Bill and his business partner that they were being sued for $1 million for allegedly stealing the technology and selling it as their own. This had not been the case, but the company had a couple of options: fight an expensive lawsuit or shut down the business. Bill's business partner left, saying, "I'm not going to fight. It's going to cost us more than we're worth." Bill now had a fledgling business and a lawsuit to contend with on his own.

Of course, he was afraid. Bill stood to lose his business, the suit, and his reputation. But he refused to let fear guide his decisions. He recalled the words of author Napoleon Hill: "Every adversity has within it the seed of an equal or greater benefit." He decided to look for the seed of benefit in his adversity.

Bill sat himself down and wrote out a list of the possible good that could come out of being sued. Topping his list: "Somebody thinks my business is worth $1 million!" Other ideas included: "Maybe I'll learn something about the law" and "I could learn more about copyright."

After two days, Bill's list contained sixty-two ideas. Had he panicked and given in to fear, these ideas could not have come to him. But because he was thinking bravely by acknowledging his fear *and* remaining open to the potential good that could come from his situation, Bill had a flood of ideas. One was to document how he had developed his business, which he had started in his kitchen. Instead of spending the time, money, and energy to fight a lawsuit, he wrote a letter to the person suing him, enclosing this documentation, and explaining his side of the story. Within a short time, the plaintiff dropped the lawsuit.

Today, nearly two hundred million people throughout the world have used programs from the Centerpointe Research Institute. Bill Harris was a consummate Brave Thinker. When he passed away in 2018, I had the honor of officiating at his service.

Befriend Your Fear

As I mentioned earlier, the point is not to rid yourself of fear. The fear you suppress only grows larger. But you can get better acquainted with fear by thinking bravely. Becoming more attuned to your senses will help you identify fear so you can deal with it directly: "I know you, Fear. I know this doubt. I know this feeling. You can accompany me, but I will not let you guide my life." Accept fear as your companion, not your master. Then shift your attention by reminding yourself that you have another companion far more formidable than fear. Tell yourself, "There is something in me greater than this fear. That something is the power guiding this universe. And when I allow it in, that power guides my life."

By contrast, Common-Hour Thinking brings the negative into the "now," exacerbating your fear, and pushes the positive into an uncertain and far-off future. Common-Hour Thinking focuses on what is probable. It sets limitations based on your circumstances and relies on your prior experience and unhealthy paradigms to devise answers. Common-Hour Thinking allows fear to grow bigger than your believing, blocking the path to your dream.

Brave Thinking requires you to face your fears and befriend them. If you attempt to rid yourself of fear, you are in for a lifelong, exhausting battle. Making fear your companion takes courage and propels your dreams.

**To create a life you truly love living, you
must train yourself in how to feel
fear and *still* act toward your dream.**

Throughout your lifetime, you've done many things
for the first time. For example, there was the first time you
kissed someone. You probably felt some fear about kissing
this person, but you did it anyway because you wanted the
experience. And what about the first time you spoke pub-
licly? I still remember speaking to my sixth-grade class, my
knees shaking under my skirt so badly I was sure my class-
mates could see.

Every one of us experiences fear, whether it is the adrenaline after a close call while driving, the butterflies in our
stomach before a big job interview, or the anxiety of being
let go from work. Anyone who dares to dream knows fear.
Endeavoring to make your dream reality requires you to
step beyond the borders of that fear. By definition, your
dream lies outside your comfort zone. Fear is what you
experience when you bump up against the edge of your
comfort zone and keep going. To create a life you truly love
living, you must train yourself in how to feel fear and *still*
act toward your dream.

That's precisely what Kim Luret did. She called her life
"one giant Gordian Knot that was impossible to untangle."
In her twenties, Kim had been a highly successful runway

model for the designers Versace and Dior. Later, she took a position in a modeling agency to recruit models, working up to sixty hours a week in what she called a "high-pressure and toxic" environment. She would arrive home about eight in the evening and after dinner, dishes, and housework, fall into bed physically and emotionally exhausted, only to get up a few hours later and return to work.

Kim longed to start her own business but didn't dare to chase that dream. She was the primary breadwinner for her husband and two teenage children, and the family could not keep up with the bills. Her job didn't pay enough to make ends meet, so she borrowed against high-interest credit cards and maxed them out. Before long, Kim was drowning in debt. "I felt trapped and terrified," she said. "The end of each month was a very scary struggle." One month, the electric company would turn off power; the next month, the phone company would cut its service. Sometimes both happened at once.

Kim's family was evicted from one apartment then another. "Every time there was a knock on the door, I would feel a sickening dread shoot through me, terrified that on the other side was someone delivering another eviction notice, or coming to take our furniture away again," she said. "I lived in a nearly constant state of fear and anxiety." By day Kim had heart palpitations. By night she lay awake in a cold sweat, consumed with worry about what was coming next. This had gone on for sixteen years.

Kim was also unhappy in her marriage and wanted a divorce. Her children became angry at her, and their once warm and loving relationship fell apart. "When I entered a room, they would get up and leave," she said. "I felt like a pariah in my own home." Kim stayed in the marriage to repair the relationship with her children because, as she put it, "without that, life wasn't worth living to me."

Finally, Kim bravely decided that she could no longer live in sorrow. To pursue her dream of starting her own business, she attended one of my DreamBuilder seminars but was terrified of spending her scant dollars on furthering that dream. Although she felt sick to her stomach, another part of her experienced a calm knowing. "I knew that if I caved into fear, I would never climb out of that dark hole that I was living in," she said. By accepting fear as her companion she could visualize the life that she loved, which included a happy marriage and a restored relationship with her children. Kim mustered the courage to trust that her dream life was possible, accepting fear as part of her life-changing journey.

She divorced her husband and ultimately became closer with him than she was during much of their marriage. She remarried a man she calls "Mr. Wonderful." Most importantly, the relationship with her children has healed. And her business success as a life coach has afforded her the time and money freedom to travel with her family. "Before I lived almost every waking moment in stress, fear, and anxiety," she said. "Now I live almost every moment in calm, peace, and joy."

Turn Common-Hour Thinking Into Brave Thinking

My adult children and I found ourselves at a standoff. We were on a long-awaited vacation in Mexico, and they wanted to rent ATVs and race through the sand dunes of

Cabo San Lucas. ATVs scared me. I could imagine all kinds of accidents and didn't plan to be in one of them. Finally, outvoted, I climbed aboard and clumsily learned to shift gears. The road leading to the dunes was plagued by potholes. I lurched while my companions glided. I was in the back of the line of eight four-wheelers, and my youngest son, Mat, kept turning around and saying, "Hurry up. You're holding up the whole group. Step on the gas."

By the time we reached the dunes, the supposed start of our journey, I'd had enough. The sand felt slippery beneath my wheels. "That was plenty for me," I said. "You guys go ahead."

One by one my grown children reiterated the teachings I had instilled in them since they were little. "Do not let fear run your life," they reminded me. It was one affirmation after another until I relented.

Downhill felt fine. I coasted. But as the others rose gracefully on hills of sand, I dug in like a gopher. The engine roared, but I could not drive upward. Obviously, I'd been given a defective ATV. Everyone kept yelling back at me to try this and try that, but nothing worked. Finally, my son-in-law, Jorge, turned off his ATV and walked over to where I sat spewing sand. So as not to embarrass me, he whispered, "Momma Mary, you have power you are not using. Take your foot off the brake."

"Oh."

Here I was, flooring the gas pedal with my foot on the brake at the same time. No wonder I couldn't move. In my fear, I was unconsciously pressing the brake, stifling the power of the ATV. By simply removing my foot from the brake, I was no longer stuck. I could climb any hill. I could explore these beautiful dunes.

Finally, I began to enjoy myself. When I allowed the vehicle to work the way it was intended, I felt more in control than I had when I unwittingly attempted to protect myself from danger.

This was classic Common-Hour Thinking. I wanted to go forward, but fear literally held me back. I couldn't see beyond my circumstances. "The ATV must be defective; therefore, I am stuck."

Because of fear of the unknown, when we want to move forward in our dream-building, we often unconsciously have one foot on the gas and the other foot on the "brake" of our personal power. We get stalled by fearful thoughts, never stopping to ask, "How am I holding back?"

Do you want a more meaningful marriage but hesitate to speak openly to your spouse? Do you dream of starting your own business but spend time imagining pitying looks and awkward whispered conversations should the business fail? "Poor guy, he's just not cut out for business."

Brave Thinking requires us to acknowledge our fear, accept it as a companion on our journey, and keep moving forward. My son-in-law's words continue to resonate with me. "You have power you are not using. Take your foot off the brake."

We often unconsciously have one foot on the gas and the other foot on the "brake" of our personal power. We get stalled by fearful thoughts, never stopping to ask, "How am I holding back?"

In our search for self-development and personal growth, let us remember that we all have the power within us to create a life we truly love. Don't let fear hold you back from fully immersing yourself in this wonderful experience called life! Take your foot off the brake and unleash the full power that's within you to move toward what you desire and deserve.

I have seen many people sabotage their dream with Common-Hour Thinking, especially when it comes to finding a soulmate—something many of my clients are seeking. They focus more on their fear of winding up alone—forever—than on the relationship they yearn to have.

Imagine your own dream is being challenged by fear. Let's say you envision your greater self as part of a twosome. Your dream is for a loving, nurturing relationship. Yet as hard as you try, that kind of bond eludes you. "Have faith," your friends tell you. "Someone will come along." Easy for them to say, you think. But what if you took that advice literally? What would you need to do?

You could start by expressing love right where you are. Shower friends and family with love at this moment. Send your parents or best friends cards telling them what they mean to you. Practice random acts of kindness to strangers. Bake cookies for the new neighbors. When you're at the supermarket, ask the grocery clerks about their day. Become a living example that love exists. This is not easy. If you haven't had a decent date in a year, loneliness can eat at your insides like acid. Brave Thinking empowers you to both acknowledge your fear and embody your dream.

The problem is that so many of us withhold our love thinking we'll wait until a prospective partner materializes.

When nobody appears, our loneliness can make us stingy with the people who do care for us—especially if we resent their being in a happy relationship. Common-Hour Thinking tells us we have every right to resent those in a happy relationship and encourages us to hoard our love.

Now suppose Mr. or Ms. Right does finally appear. You nab this prospective mate before they can get away. You pour out your pent-up love so eagerly that you convey not celebration but desperation. And that person goes, "Whoa!" and gets scared off. Either that, or despairing of meeting anyone decent, you grab the next available person who comes along, blind yourself to any red flags, and wind up settling for a poor facsimile of your dream.

Turn the tables for a moment: When someone else is looking for love, do you find their clinging to you for dear life particularly attractive, or even flattering?

There is a law of attraction in this universe: The universe responds in kind to the energy you generate. Those who love life are loved back. People in satisfying relationships radiate a loving confidence that draws to them even more warmth. Brave Thinking asks you to be loving and nurturing right where you stand.

Don't get me wrong. Loneliness so profound that it physically hurts to see a pair of strangers holding hands cannot be trivialized. You long for what others seem to take for granted. Generating love toward others may not whisk a soulmate into your life right away; but if you live lovingly, you will attract other loving people to your life. Through the law of attraction, we are always attracting to us what is in harmony with our desire and our expectations. This is true in all four quadrants of life: health and well-being, love and relationships, vocation, and time and money freedom. In her job as modeling recruiter, Kim Luret worked long hours but had virtually no time or money freedom, living in fear that the power or phone would be turned off once again. When she bravely decided to pursue her dream of becoming a life coach, her income grew substantially, and she had the freedom to travel with her family.

To better understand the role Common-Hour Thinking plays in fear, consider these *Time* magazine cover headlines:

- "World Money Crisis"

- "Inefficiency in America: Why Nothing Seems to Work Any More"

- "The Crash: After a Wild Week on Wall Street, the World Is Different"

- "Is the U.S. Going Broke?"

- "War in the Middle East"

- "The Polluted Air"

- "Our Filthy Seas"

- "The Energy Mess"

- "What's Wrong with U.S. Medicine"

It's hard not to feel fearful when we are inundated by news that portends disaster for our economy, environment, health, and security. Does "the crash" on Wall Street mean I'll lose the money I've invested in retirement and wind up working the rest of my life? Will pollution make our planet unhabitable for our children and grandchildren? These conversations are taking place all over the world today; however, these cover stories are more than thirty-five years old. We are still talking about the Middle East and about the air and about economic problems in the United States. This is because, as a people, we stay in the same conversation, which keeps us in the same vibration, creating the same results over and over. As a nation and as individuals we need to replace Common-Hour Thinking with Brave Thinking if we are to progress as a country and as individuals. Frightening headlines exacerbate our fear and they do not help us to envision and create a better future.

Here are some concrete examples of Common-Hour Thinking versus Brave Thinking. Can you see how to switch from one to the other?

Common-Hour Thinking: "I need to wait for the right time before I do this. I don't have time to do that right now."

Brave Thinking: "I make time for the things that matter most in my life. We all get twenty-four hours. We all make time for what we decide we're going to make time for. I make time for the things that matter most to me."

Common-Hour Thinking: "What will others think?"

Brave Thinking: "I am the highest authority on what's right for me."

Common-Hour Thinking: "I should wait until I have the whole plan before I move forward."

Brave Thinking: "What can I do from where I am with what I have that will move me in the direction of my dream?"

Common-Hour Thinking is contractive; Brave Thinking is expansive. Only when you have a direction in mind can you advance toward it. You can step inside your dream as a living experience and transmit it into the minds of others. Imagining this puts you on a different frequency. And then, as Thoreau wrote, "new, universal, and more liberal laws" establish themselves around you. The old laws are rearranged in your favor. You are becoming a Brave Thinker.

I want to close this chapter with one of my heroes, Rosa Parks, whose refusal to give up her seat on the bus changed the course of history. For years, I had wondered how, on that pivotal day of December 1, 1955, did this Brave Thinker find the inner strength to defy the bus driver who repeatedly ordered her to relinquish her seat to a white passenger who had just come on board. Parks was arrested for violating the segregation law that dictated Black passengers had to give up their seats for white passengers. Her courageous act and subsequent arrest ignited the Montgomery Bus Boycott, a key event in the civil rights movement that ultimately ended Jim Crow segregation. But for Parks personally, it also meant death threats, unemployment, and poverty. Her act of civil disobedience defied more than just a bus driver. It challenged a deeply entrenched power system built on a long history of bigotry and oppression.

Decades later, the United Nations began hosting an annual celebration that came to be called the Gandhi-King Season for Nonviolence, honoring the philosophies of Mohandas Gandhi and Dr. Martin Luther King Jr. Season for Nonviolence is also a national sixty-four-day grassroots awareness campaign focused on obtaining peace through nonviolent action. As the president of the Association for

Global New Thought, and with a longstanding relationship with this work, I had been invited to speak for a third time at the United Nations event in 2000. During a break in the presentations, Rosa Parks and I were both on the dais. I turned to her and asked how she had found the inner strength to defy that system of racism and bigotry. A whole row of Black passengers was ordered to move to the back because one white man came on the bus. The rest obeyed. But Parks did not, even though she knew there would be swift and potentially terrifying consequences.

"What happened inside of you?" I asked.

She took a breath and said, "There comes a moment in all of us when we want to know our own dignity. I believed it was God's law. Martin Luther King told us how he had trained all the freedom workers in the practice of nonviolence, knowing that they would be hit and beaten. But he also told them that soul force is greater than brutality, that eventually love will have its way. Love is a stronger force than hate, and either you believe that, or you don't believe it.

"I believed it," she said. "And this was my moment."

EXERCISE: Finding Good in a Fearful Situation

Recall a time when something happened that caused you to become fearful. Now that this situation is behind you, can you think of any good that came out of your experience? If so, write it down. Make a list. Are you stronger, more resilient? Today, as a budding dream builder, you are challenged to step out of your comfort zone, which can also provoke fearful thoughts. For example, you may wonder, "What if I haven't got what it takes?" Then look for the potential good.

Review the list you just composed. You don't have to wait for fear to subside before taking the brave step of looking for the good.

COMMON-HOUR THINKING VERSUS BRAVE THINKING

Brave Thinking Tool: Pause and look for any possible good
Press pause on the panic that can arise when something seemingly bad happens and turn your attention to what possible good could come from this challenge.

Teaching points
- Befriend your fear, accepting it as a traveling companion as you move outside your comfort zone and toward your dream.

- Turn Common-Hour Thinking into Brave Thinking, leaning into the truth that you are always more powerful than your conditions.

Exercise
- List all of the good that came out of a situation from your past that initially caused you to become fearful. How did you turn that challenge into a benefit, and how are you more aware, stronger, or even more resilient now as result?

6

THE COURAGE
TO COMMIT

"Where the Mind goes Energy flows."

ERNEST HOLMES

———————————

I dictate results.

I am responsible for

The thoughts that I think.

———————————

F YOU WANT to transform a substance, you need sufficient energy to get from one phase to another. Think
about boiling water. By turning the burner to high, you
put enough energy into the water to eventually reach the
boiling point of 212 degrees Fahrenheit. From personal
experience, however, I can tell you that when I'm chilled
and want a cup of tea right this minute, the water just sits
there. No steam. No bubbles. Nothing. If you stand over the
stove and watch water heat up, you might think nothing is
changing for a long time. This is how dream-building works:
you can exert tremendous energy but still think nothing is
working because you haven't seen the results yet. In fact,
you just haven't crossed the energy threshold. Pressure is
building. Change may be right around the corner, but there
isn't sufficient energy yet. What's needed is just a little more
attention—to turn up the temperature, so to speak, just a
few more degrees.

This process is not about getting *to* your dream. That's
impossible, because your dream doesn't exist yet, not in the
physical realm at least. It is, in a way, calling to you *from*
the infinite space of possibility, from the quantum realm,

where all potentialities exist. In both the quantum and the conscious world, observation creates reality. In other words, nothing is real until you observe it. Quantum physics is an invisible world where matter and energy are in constant flux, transforming back and forth between energy fields and particles such as electrons. Quantum theory states that until someone focuses on a particle, it does not exist in any one location. And so it is in the conscious world.

When you think about your environment, career, relationships, or health, you make choices about what to observe, and by merely observing, your observation becomes reality. For example, imagine you are at home, looking out the window on a crisp fall day. As the wind picks up, hundreds of crimson leaves flutter to the ground. If you observe the leaves as nature's glory, the reality is that your view is beautiful. If you choose to observe those leaves as something that requires raking—a chore you abhor, especially after heavy rain—your world becomes filled with drudgery instead of delight. Until you focus on either reality, neither exists. By simply opening your mind to abundance, health, love, and joy you are more likely to observe those realities. Through your observation, you can see the beautiful fall display or the drudgery of dead leaves.

Jim Carrey is a prime example of extreme focus and commitment.

Early in his career, the actor wrote himself a check for $10 million and gave himself three years to cash it, dating the check for Thanksgiving of 1995. In the notation, he wrote, "For acting services rendered." At the time, the Canadian comedian was just another unknown who had moved to Los Angeles to pursue his dream of becoming an actor.

BRAVE THINKING TOOL

I am responsible
for two things:
(1) the thoughts I think and
(2) the actions I take

Each night, Carrey would drive up Mulholland Drive into the Hollywood Hills and gaze down at the city, imagining his dream as if it had already come true. As he told Oprah Winfrey in an interview, "I would visualize having directors interested in me, people that I respected saying, 'I like your work.'" At the time, he was broke. The check in his wallet began to deteriorate, but the process of imagining a future he wanted to embody motivated him to succeed. He was determined. "You can't just visualize and go eat a sandwich," he told Oprah.

Carrey was using his own version of the Brave Thinking Tool that states, "I am responsible for two things: (1) the thoughts I think and (2) the actions I take." Carrey had clearly identified his dream, then laser-focused his attention on visualizing himself living his dream as if it had already happened. He committed to the dream by boldly writing himself a $10 million check, holding on to it for years while he pursued his craft.

When you place your attention on your dream, do it with the state of mind of having already realized that dream, and proceed from that point. If you're skeptical, your attention wanders, and your dream won't have the same power. Feeling the emotion of this future "accomplishment," Carrey acted *from* his dream instead of trying to move *toward* it. And it worked. He was paid $7 million for his role in 1994 film *Dumb and Dumber*. Carrey would go on to become the first actor ever to make $20 million on a single film, which he received for his role in *The Cable Guy* in 1996. When we nourish our dreams with attention, they grow.

Where do you focus your attention? In our busy, multitasking lives we can find ourselves attempting to mentally attend to so many things at once that we wind up focusing on none. Buddhists call the chattering mind a jumping monkey. At any given time, you are running through a myriad of thoughts, perhaps about what happened before, what's going to happen later, what to have for dinner, who will pick up the dry cleaning, and so-and-so's hurtful remark about you. Thoughts may race at a hundred miles an hour, yet you can learn to tether and calm your mind. Just because a thought enters your awareness doesn't mean you have to feed it with your attention.

You learn to focus your attention by mentally stepping into your dream, again and again. Unfortunately, we've had more practice imagining worst-case scenarios than visualizing ourselves in the life we would love. A woman I know imagines her husband having an affair, or worse still, lying in a ditch, whenever he isn't home from work on time. If you place your attention on your problem—real or imaginary—you will contract, as though shrinking or folding in on yourself. You might even slump or slouch when imagining how this problem weighs you down. You may feel discouraged, even helpless. Whereas when you place your attention on your dream, you expand. Try it right now. Can you feel the excitement in your body, almost like an internal buzzing? Expect that the universe knows how to bring your dream to fruition. If you have no expectation, then that desire just stays in the domain of wishing, wanting, or daydreaming and will never reveal itself. The law of attraction states that we are always attracting to us what is in harmony with our desire and our expectations. But many of us have learned to expect little. We have learned to expect struggle. We have learned to expect barely getting by. As you evoke higher expectations, connect that to the powerful force of attention. Your thinking drives your behavior, which drives your results. Those results create new environments that will ultimately influence your thinking. If you want better results, change your thinking. And as you move from one life to the next, be strategic about your attention—focus on where you're headed, not on where you've been.

When you focus your attention, you direct energy. Unless you consciously intend for your dream to become reality, you unconsciously intend that something else takes form. Your very nature directs energy. We make countless choices every single day based on where we place our attention. Deciding what to eat, what to wear, or whether to pay the electric bill instead of the water bill affects our lives in ways large and small. Our emotions, relationships, home, career—every part of our lives springs forth from attention. We will experience all these aspects of our lives, but how we experience them is in our hands as a cocreator with the Infinite. The only things we totally control are the thoughts we think, the thoughts we nurture.

In the first part of this book—"Blueprinting"—you used the power of your imagination to identify a dream that is a deep longing of yours. You did not render your dreams puny by crossing out what you truly desire, nor did you edit your heart by telling yourself, "What I really want is impossible. Maybe I should just settle for..." You tapped into your deep longing and recognized yourself as worthy of a life you would love. The likelihood of a dream coming true is based less on what logic dictates than on your willingness to form a vision, to risk, to step beyond your current experience.

Bridging is the art of mentally moving from your old life into the new one.

As you can see, our old friend "Notice what you are noticing" was just the beginning. It is a tool that helps you to follow your thoughts and be conscious of them, and you will notice when your thoughts are wandering from your intention. With this skill the next step is to direct your thoughts.

When you need to pound in a nail and you are holding it in place with one hand to start, there is only one right place to look—at the head of the nail. If you focus on that, odds are you will hit the nail on the head. If you look at your thumb, you'll most likely hit the nail of your thumb. When your mind goes on autopilot and your attention wanders, you wind up with bent nails, a smashed thumb, or an unintended life.

Focus is what you do in the moment. Committing is holding that focus. When you focus your attention, you direct energy. Committing is the pledge or promise you make to yourself to keep the energy flowing. Committing means holding that focus for as long as necessary—a few seconds for pounding a nail, and months or years for building your dream business.

When committing to yourself or to someone else, you are creating trust. You are putting your integrity on the line. If you commit to taking care of the neighbor's dog while they're on vacation, and the neighbors come home to an unhappy pup, you have breached their trust. A lot of times we don't want to commit because, if we don't live up to our word, we risk compromising our integrity. To risk letting ourselves down requires courage. Commitment is Brave Thinking. Building your dream, however, is not dog sitting.

It is not a short-term, well-defined endeavor. When you commit to a dream, you may not have all the facts. As you learn, you adjust your commitments accordingly.

We've all heard the expression "keep your eye on the ball." I have been inspired watching slow-motion videos of the great Roger Federer hitting a tennis ball. His full attention is riveted to the point where the ball and racket connect. Even as the rest of his body pivots to put tremendous force into the shot, his head and eyes do not move. Many players are so anxious to see if the ball is going where they hoped it would, they take their eyes off it, and the ball lands out of bounds or in the net.

As you begin to build the bridge between the blueprint of your dreams and a brand-new life, you will continue to notice what you are noticing. Every thought has a frequency. If you hold your focus and just keep breathing for 365 days, three years in a row, you're going to have results, because you *must* think. You are always going to be thinking. No options about that; there is no stasis when it comes to thinking. But most people do not notice *what* they are thinking or *that* they are thinking. As you become more aware, you assume your place in the driver's seat of your life.

When you decide on your dream and really commit to a life you would love, you begin a phase change. Water boils when it has sufficient energy, transforming it into a different state. You, too, enter a different state when you have committed sufficient energy to your dream. That dream now exists not only in your mind but in your hands and your life. Fueled by your commitment, the dream moves toward fruition. Commitment takes courage. If your decision is wobbly, the floundering energy cannot be used to focus on the opportunities available to you. "Maybe I will" or "maybe I won't" language won't allow you to build anything new.

William H. Murray was a highly respected Scottish mountain climber who knew something about commitment—and courage. As a young man, he climbed some of the world's tallest mountains. As a soldier in World War II, he was captured and spent three years in prisoner of war camps. While in a German prison camp, using the only thing he could find—rough toilet paper—he wrote a philosophical book about mountain climbing. The Gestapo discovered his manuscript and promptly destroyed it. When Murray began to write the book a second time, again on toilet paper, his fellow prisoners were amazed. The odds of his succeeding were almost nil. Murray's health had deteriorated because of near starvation. He didn't know if he would ever be strong enough to climb again. And should the Nazis find his second manuscript, he knew they would destroy it in an instant. And yet, both Murray and his book survived. Emaciated after the war, Murray spent two years rebuilding his strength. *Mountaineering in Scotland* was published in 1947, rekindling national interest in mountain climbing. Murray himself went on to complete three landmark Himalayan expeditions, including one that paved the way for Sir Edmund Hillary's milestone ascent of Mount Everest in 1953. Murray spent his later years as an environmentalist, determined to protect the Scottish Highlands that so inspired him. I have long been inspired by Murray and his philosophy about commitment, which he described in his autobiography, *The Evidence of Things Not Seen,* which was published in 2002, several years after his death. The book's title comes from a line in the New Testament:

"Faith is the evidence of things not seen." This is my favorite passage from the book:

> Until one is committed, there is hesitancy, the chance to draw back, always ineffectiveness. Concerning all acts of initiative (and creation), there is one elementary truth, the ignorance of which kills countless ideas and splendid plans: that the moment one definitely commits oneself, then Providence moves too. All sorts of things occur to help one that would never otherwise have occurred. A whole stream of events issues from the decision, raising in one's favour all manner of unforeseen incidents and meetings and material assistance, which no man could have dreamt would have come his way... "Whatever you can do, or dream you can, begin it. Boldness has genius, power, and magic in it."

Beware the Drift

So, where are you now? You have dreamed a beautiful dream by asking yourself, "What would I love?" When you put yourself inside that dream, you feel more alive. You have tested that dream, weighed and considered it and conditioned yourself to look for the good when a seemingly bad situation threatens what you deeply desire, trusting that good things show up for those who focus, commit, and expect them.

What can go wrong?

For starters, at some point you'll get distracted. The biggest danger to your dream is what's called "drift." You drift into old patterns, drift into busyness, drift into the whirlwind of your daily life. But this is your moment to claim your spot in your dream. Something I know in my bones to be true after more than forty years of study and experience is that the Infinite does not read your intention. It reads your attention. Where you place your attention communicates a vibration. The Infinite picks this up and matches your frequency.

The Book of Judges in the Old Testament tells the story of Samson, who was blessed with a gift of strength that was not of this world. Samson's might was so immense that the Israelites depended on him to defend them against the oppressive Philistines. But like many of us, Samson got caught in the drift.

Tired of fighting a losing battle, the Philistines sent a beautiful seductress named Delilah to coax Samson into revealing the secret of his strength. He toyed with her, professing that if he was bound with new ropes, he would be rendered as weak as the next guy. So Delilah arranged to have Samson bound, and naturally he broke through the ropes as if they were string. Delilah kept trying to entice the truth from him, but Samson just kept showing off.

At some point, you would think Samson would figure it out: "This woman is bad news." But no. That is one reason I like this story so much. We all tend to miss cues and let ourselves be led astray from our dreams.

One night, after being pestered relentlessly, Samson blurted out, "If my head is shaved, then my strength will leave me, and I shall become weak and be like any other man." Delilah wasted no time. After lulling Samson to sleep, she cut his hair and arranged to have him turned him over to the Philistines. They plucked out his eyes, hauled him off to prison, and harnessed him to the millstone to grind grain.

Samson's story is a metaphor for every dream builder. For one reason or another, most of us stray off course. We lose our vision. And if we allow ourselves to be distracted with the Delilahs in our lives, we can wind up living at the millstone, going round and round, getting nowhere.

But here is the good news. Samson's hair started to grow back. He pulled down the Philistine's temple. In our lives, we all have Delilahs that can tempt us to drift from our dreams. Delilahs can doll themselves up in some pretty alluring disguises, and because they are so seductive, we often don't recognize them for what they are: fear, distraction, doubt, confusion, and procrastination. For example, we immerse ourselves in the next big work project, even though we dream of a new career. Or we spend yet another evening with our friend Netflix, even as we yearn for camaraderie with actual human beings. When we start to doubt our abilities, time, or resources to manifest our dream, we can allow fear to busy our fingers or numb our minds, leaving us no energy to build the reality that we would love.

In this process, you will surely encounter distraction, doubt, and procrastination. As you bridge the gap between your dream and a life you would love, remember this process takes time. It takes perseverance to see through whatever obstacles present themselves. Problems cannot be solved by the same level of thinking that created them. As you experience challenges in building your dream, beware the drift. You strengthen your resolve by committing.

Commit to your dream mentally, emotionally, and spiritually. We break commitments all the time, disappointing others as well as ourselves. For your dream to manifest, you've got to stick with it, pledging yourself to a particular course of action. As you commit you willingly step toward your dream, proceeding even as doubts arise. As you experience drift, you honor your commitment to yourself by getting back on track. The universe can do for you only what it can do through you. You have been given the capacity to grow whatever life you choose. The Infinite is powerful, but it can't steer a parked car. The act of commitment builds a path to your dreams, bringing you little successes along the way. Support that you cannot create for yourself will come to you through your willingness to be guided by the Infinite.

Turn a Want Into a Must

Inspiration without action is merely entertainment. When I was diagnosed with terminal kidney disease, naturally I wanted to get better. But not until the night before my surgery, with the chaplain at my bedside, did that want become a must. With the chaplain's guidance, I put the imperative into action, envisioning my infant son in a future that included both of us: I was walking him to his first day of kindergarten; watching with pride as he received his high school diploma; and beaming with joy as he married the woman of his dreams.

Inspiration without action

is merely entertainment.

When my son Mat was in high school, he dreamed of playing college football. But when a college football marketing specialist visited his school, he said there was no way he could represent Mat to the college recruiting scouts. At his height and speed, Mat was a dime a dozen. Thousands of kids coming out of high school were just like him. He wasn't anything special.

When someone looks you up and down and says, "No, I don't think you have what it takes," you have two options. You can either agree with that doubt, or you can agree with the divine in you and go for what you would love. In that moment, Mat recognized the one thing that distinguished him from all the other players: he could outwork them.

He spent the summer after his senior year at the gym and running sprints on the field for hours and hours every day. As a result, he made the University of San Diego, Division 1-AA football team. He was the fourth string running back and third string on the kickoff team, but he dreamed of getting on the field.

About halfway through the season, his brothers, John and Rich, decided they would fly out to watch him play. John and Rich had not played college football, and they were eager to support Mat. The only problem? Mat had yet to see the field. And he didn't want his brothers to get on a plane just to watch him sit on a bench.

Mat thought he had been giving it his all before, but in anticipation of his brothers' visit, now at every practice he was the last one off the field, sprinting to every drill, hitting as hard as he could, and hoping the coaches would see that little Mat Boggs was someone to take seriously. But when the team starters list was posted each week, Mat's name was still not on it. During practice the week before his brother's visit, however, he noticed the kickoff team was not performing well. Frustrated, the coach barked at the team, "I want you to go out there and become a kamikaze!" The team still lost their game that week.

With his brothers arriving the next weekend, Mat desperately wanted to get onto the field. That the kickoff team was not in kamikaze mode made him think he had a shot. He asked himself, "What can I do?" And he looked toward the Infinite for guidance. In the meantime, he showed up even earlier for practice and practiced even harder. When the charts went up that Thursday, there was Mat's name, still on the bench.

Come game day, Saturday, he kept replaying the question: "What can I do?" When the game started, he looked to the stands, saw his brothers watching, and felt something happen. His desire shifted. It went from a *want* to a *must*.

Before a change can occur, you need sufficient energy to initiate the transformation. Many of us sit on the sidelines of life wanting something without generating sufficient energy to achieve it. We don't want it badly enough. But when your dream goes from a want to a must, everything changes. And in that moment, on that Saturday, that's what happened with Mat's dream. He needed to be a kamikaze, a word that translates as "the wind of gods" or "divine wind."

Suddenly, Mat had a brave idea. He knew it was brave because fear rocketed through his entire body. He could stand up and say, "Hey, Coach. You want a kamikaze? I'm your man." The Common-Hour Thinking part of him balked. This was a risky move. The coach could put him in his place, and he would be humiliated. Mat was a freshman.

That meant his job was to sit down and shut up. He had not yet earned his place on the field. He even worried about getting kicked off the team for being out of line, because that's what Common-Hour Thinking does. It prescribes us a role and then we spend the rest of our own lives warming the bench.

Mat didn't have a lot of time to ruminate. He stood up and said, "Hey, Coach. If you want a kamikaze, I'm your man."

On the next kickoff, the coach gave Mat a chance. Mat sprinted down the field and tackled the receiver. For the rest of his college career, he played first string.

You must claim your spot for your dream. If you're willing to claim it, say it. Write it down, speak it aloud, make it your own. Moving from a want to a must is your moment of commitment. Unless you are committed to your dream, over time your energy wanes. Invest yourself emotionally by keeping your passion alive. If you maintain enthusiasm for your dream, you will draw greater inspiration and substance to it. You remain pliable, knowing doors will open in the form of new opportunities and fresh guidance. Your commitment to be molded moves you into the space where your dream can come true.

Resonate with Your Vision Daily

Andrew Carnegie was an industrialist and philanthropist who spent the first half of his life earning vast amounts of money and the second half giving it away. He believed that all people, regardless of socioeconomic status, should have access to a quality education.

Napoleon Hill was a young journalist with little formal education. As a child, he ran wild, often brandishing a pistol, until his stepmother persuaded him to replace the pistol with a typewriter.

Imagine how Hill felt being granted a three-hour interview with Carnegie, then the richest man in the world. My colleague and friend, the late Bob Proctor, was fascinated by the relationship between these two men. He shared with me and others a remarkable story from the Napoleon Hill Foundation archives.

That three-hour interview turned into an invitation for Hill to spend the weekend at Carnegie's home. During that time, Carnegie shared his dream with Hill. His philosophy was that extremely wealthy people had a hidden pattern for success that often died with them. He was looking for a writer to spend twenty years studying the pattern, and then write a book for the masses that would give ordinary individuals the opportunity to achieve extraordinary success. He knew Hill was the man for the job.

The plan was simple: Hill would invest twenty years in studying success, and Carnegie would pave the way through various introductions and connections to five hundred self-made millionaires. The rest was up to Hill. For twenty years of work, however, Carnegie would not pay him one penny.

Hill didn't know it at the time, but Carnegie had a stopwatch hidden behind his desk. He would allow Hill only sixty seconds to say yes or no. Carnegie knew that successful people made decisions quickly, because they lived their lives being expansive not contractive. If Hill took a millisecond longer, Carnegie would rescind the offer. Hill accepted within twenty-nine seconds.

Carnegie acknowledged that twenty years of research was a tough assignment. He offered Hill a formula that he said would enable his protégé to "condition his mind so thoroughly" that nothing in the world could stop him from completing his work. At least twice a day, Hill was to look in the mirror and say, "Andrew Carnegie, not only shall I match your achievements in life, but I'll meet you at the post and I'll pass you at the grandstands." Hill found that statement preposterous, but he agreed.

Hill did as Carnegie asked. Twice a day, he repeated that phrase aloud to himself while looking in the mirror. At first, he was scared. Hill shared an apartment with his brother. He didn't want his brother to see him making a fool of himself. So he'd go into the bathroom, close the door tight, and whisper the words Carnegie had given him. He said he felt like "a fool, a thief" for going through this farce.

After about a week, however, something inside him shifted. He decided to change his attitude. After all, if Carnegie chose him, that great man must have seen something that Hill had not seen in himself. Hill continued to resonate with his vision daily.

Over twenty years, he studied five hundred self-made millionaires, including Carnegie. Hill's most famous book, *Think and Grow Rich*, is one of the top-selling books of the last century and has fueled the success of countless millionaires. Hill's philosophy was that belief plays a powerful role in an individual's success. As he wrote, "Whatever the mind can conceive and believe, the mind can achieve regardless of how many times you may have failed in the past and no matter how lofty your aims and hopes may be."

Resonate with your vision every day. Napoleon Hill whispered into the mirror so his brother wouldn't overhear him. Jim Carrey drove up into the Hollywood Hills night after night, looking down at the city as he envisioned movie directors telling him, "I like your work." This technique is not just for iconic authors and movie stars. All of us are responsible for two things: our thoughts and our actions. Nourish your dream with attention, strengthen your commitment, turning your want into a must, and stay focused. As Thoreau instructed us, endeavor to live the life you have imagined and you, too, will "meet with a success unexpected in common hours" and truly love living your life. With a Brave Thinking mindset, you will not only equal your past achievements but meet yourself at the post and pass yourself at the grandstands.

THE COURAGE TO COMMIT

Brave Thinking Tool: I am responsible for two things:
(1) the thoughts I think and (2) the actions I take
Your thoughts generate feelings that lead to the actions that you do or do not take, determining the results you achieve in your life.

Teaching points

- Beware the drift, as old patterns and the whirlwind of daily life can set in, creating distraction, and pushing your vision to the backburner.

- Turn a want into a must by committing to your dream mentally, emotionally, and spiritually.

- Resonate with your vision daily by vividly imagining yourself living that dream life as if it is your current reality.

TRANSFORMING THE PAIN OF THE PAST

*"Success is not final, failure is not fatal:
it is the courage to continue that counts."*

WINSTON CHURCHILL

———————

Real transformation

Is only one thought away,

Good/bad/otherwise.

———————

HAVE EARNED TWO black belts: one in what I've learned through success and the other in what failure has taught me. Everyone experiences failure; it is a given in any life journey, especially when building a dream. In your quest to embody the life you love, you *will* fail at some juncture. It's important to expect this and know what you'll do when failure comes knocking. You have the power to turn any failure into a stepping stone.

Easy for me to say this now, but when my own moment of reckoning came, I was ill prepared.

I have shared my story with you about becoming a pregnant teenager and getting married at age sixteen. Haven and I spent nine years in therapy trying to make our connection strong enough to stay together, and we did, for twenty-seven years. We raised four wonderful children and parted ways in mid-life. To this day, we remain good friends. We enjoy celebrating the milestones of our grandchildren, such as birthdays, graduations, and most recently, a wedding. Ours was not a failed marriage, but a completed one.

I also shared the story of Living Enrichment Center, the church of my dreams. The transition from a rented movie theater to an expansive permanent home was highly complex, and we hired a CPA who also had experience assisting church organizations with their finances. For two years, the CPA and I talked business. Then we fell in love. The evening before our wedding, we held a blending ceremony to celebrate the joining of our families, his two young children and my four young adults. Like most marriages ours had ups and downs, but I chose to focus on the positive. Life was very full. On a typical Sunday, three thousand people attended services. My previously published books had become bestsellers in their genre. I had a PBS special. I spoke at the United Nations and met with some of the great leaders of our time.

Then one day, I opened a piece of mail that changed everything.

The letter concerned a mortgage on our home that I knew nothing about. When I showed the letter to my husband, he refused to talk about it. I found other financial documents in our home that puzzled me. I thought about my inattention to the concerns of some of the church staff who questioned the Living Enrichment Center's financial statements. I began to think something must be drastically wrong. I went to outside CPAs to help me unravel what was going on.

What we discovered would be devastating.

Living Enrichment Center was the spiritual home to over four thousand people. I had personally trained twelve ministers, and our ministry was doing the transformational work I had always dreamed of on a worldwide scale. And now, $1 million had gone missing from the church. I had blindly trusted my CPA husband. I did not know about the embezzlement, but I should have known.

A federal investigation ensued.

With faith in my leadership lost, the board and I were forced to close the church. Then came the question, what do I do about the congregant loans that had enabled the church to purchase the buildings and property, loans that amounted to millions? All I could think was, "I've got to find a way to pay back our congregants." My husband pleaded guilty and served time in federal prison. With all trust in our relationship shattered, I filed for divorce.

The news media had a field day. Instead of being the Mary who made news for her work with the Dalai Lama, I was Mary, part of an embezzlement that destroyed her church. I'll never forget the headline about the minister "fleecing her flock." Although many friends and congregants stood by me, just as many did not. I could not blame them for feeling betrayed. My failure to do the very thing I preached—notice, focus, pay attention—had cost them and me dearly.

To pay the congregants back would take millions of dollars. When I heard the enormity of the debt I was overwhelmed with shame and despair. Yet from somewhere deep inside came the thought, "I'm either going to pay those millions back or I will die trying." I signed an agreement to contribute a portion of my income to retiring the debt until parishioners were repaid, or for the next twenty years.

How I would accomplish this, I had no idea. I had lost my job, had no money, and had just given my last sermon. My reputation was in tatters. I felt crushed by the weight of my failure and the havoc it was wreaking on our congregants' finances and their faith. During this time, I held myself together, hoping I could find a safe place to let go and explore the depth of my loss. I drove to the Oregon coast. Spending time by the sea and feeling my toes in the sand had always healed and soothed me. I headed for an especially quiet beach where I hoped no one would find me. As I walked that beach, crying for hours on end, I realized my pent-up grief was just beginning to surface. I needed more time on what had become my grieving ground.

I walked into a local real estate office and asked a woman sitting behind the counter, "Do you know of someone... a room... someone with a room in their house I could rent?" I was so overcome with grief and humiliation that I could barely get the words out. The woman, a real estate agent, surprised me by responding, "Oh, Mary, I'm so sorry you're going through this. You don't know me, but I've attended your women's retreats." Then she told me about a couple who had built a new house but needed three months to get their property into the rental pool. "They asked me if I could recommend someone I trusted to stay in their house and just pay the utilities," she said. "I would love for you to do that." The trust of this kind woman buoyed me at a time I was drowning. I moved to the beach.

Meanwhile, everything was being moved out of my former home. The footprint of my formerly expansive life had been reduced to footprints on the sand that were washed away each day by the incoming tide. For the following twelve weeks, I did little but walk on the beach, cry, and berate myself for taking my eye off the ball. In a commencement speech, Steve Jobs once said, "You can't connect the dots looking forward. You can only connect them looking backward."

Acknowledge Your Pain

For guidance, I turned to a poem called "Dark Night of the Soul" by a sixteenth-century mystic, St. John of the Cross. I felt like my own soul had been devoured. I had dreamed big and fallen hard, and I felt fearful of ever trying again. "Dark Night" reflected St. John's own struggles with spirituality, reminding me that when darkness falls, our first instinct is to make it go away. That is what I wanted, for the entire mess to evaporate, and my pain along with it. But that was not the lesson. The lesson was to sit with the darkness without wishing it away, to learn from it, and to see the good even in the bad. When you stop fighting and set the problem down, there is a release. And eventually, a strange feeling comes upon you, and you don't want the darkness to end too soon because you want everything it came to give you.

St. John's writings guided me at a time when I could not see my own way out. You might be in such a state right now, where everything is shrouded in darkness. I learned that this place of being unable to see what's next is no accident, nor is it bad. In fact, darkness can be restorative. "In the inner stillness where meditation leads," writes St. John, "the Spirit secretly anoints the soul and heals our deepest wounds." You have access to an Infinite source. You may partner with life, guiding its energy with your attention, but the hardest part of this journey is learning to endure when nothing seems to be happening for you. When I was walking that beach, I felt crushing sadness. I missed my job. I missed the church. I missed helping people; it was the core around which I had built my entire adult life. I loved watching as people transformed their lives and achieved their dreams.

Not only was I sad but I was angry, mostly at myself. I had not given enough attention to those at our church who had questions about the financials. I chose not to see how troubling my marriage had become. Over the course of some months, my husband had become increasingly reclusive. It should have set off alarm bells, but I kept my hands firmly pressed over my ears. I realized that I had been unconsciously fearing something that, in hindsight, seemed trivial. "What would our congregation think about having a twice-divorced minister as their leader?" This echoed back to my childhood: "What would the neighbors think?" As it turns out, fear of looking bad as a public figure has an enormous cost. But there is an advantage to hitting rock bottom that people in recovery understand better than most: you are not on this path alone. The afternoon I realized this, after five long weeks of crying, for the first time, I walked the beach without tears.

After weeks of listening to the sound of the rolling waves and feeling completely lost, I heard a still, small voice inside me—one I hadn't heard in quite some time—say to me, "Mary, you're still breathing." Sadness and grief had been broadcast so loudly within me that I had not been able to hear that other part of me, but it broke through that day. We all have a Higher Power, access to an Infinite source of energy and wisdom, full of possibility. And then the voice said, "Dark chapter. Not your whole book." That was news to me; I thought my dream-building days were over. But the thought that this could be just a chapter? That felt like hope. Amazing how a single, powerful thought can shift your perspective, even the course of your life.

I recalled a similar walk on the beach, decades earlier, when we had taken our fledgling ministry on the road, crossing the country in a blue taxi packed with four children, towing a travel trailer, and with scant cash. After paying $172 to get our brakes fixed, I got scared. We always seemed to have just enough money to put gas in the car and food on our makeshift table. At different points on our journey, Haven and I took on window-washing jobs to keep us afloat. But when we reached Florida, nobody wanted our services. Our money ebbed, until one morning we had only three dollars left. That afternoon I walked along the beach, feeling desperate about money and furious at God. This state of mind usually leads us to look down, the direction that we are headed in emotionally. I kicked angrily at the sand. I felt like I'd put my whole life on the line for the Spirit, yet my dream teetered on the verge of extinction.

I asked God for a sign that we should continue with our mobile ministry. At that moment, I saw a small, shiny object in the sand, a single penny. At one time, I would have ignored it. But the appearance of this humble coin at the very moment I requested a sign gave me faith. The universe sends out signals all the time, but we tend to overlook them. We still had a little food in the trailer, but not enough, so I took our three remaining dollars to a nearby grocery store and bought two packages of split peas, one green and one yellow, for thirty-seven cents each. The two different-colored peas would convince the kids we were having different dinners that evening and the next two.

As I reached into my pocket for a dollar bill, one of those moments of clarity we learn to recognize flashed through my mind. My still, small voice, that calm resonance that is deeper than our conscious mind, said to me, "You are tithing your time and you are tithing your talent, but you are not tithing your dollars." My experience of abundance had diminished in the one area of my life where I was holding back. I was not sharing what had been given to me financially. I counted out thirty cents of the three dollars we had that day and put it in the donations box at the chapel of the Christian campground where we had parked our trailer. Then I prayed. A few hours later, Haven returned to the campground. I braced myself for more stories of rejection. Instead, he told me a woman had paid him eighty dollars to wash her windows. We immediately took eight dollars and sent it to the church where our next workshop was scheduled. And the jobs kept coming.

It is hard to imagine that the memory of an unexpected eighty dollars comforted me at a time when I had millions of dollars to repay. But it did. That long-past time of wondering how we would feed our family was a chapter in my story about the transformative power of thinking, and of listening—to the still, small voice. I *was* still breathing. This more painful chapter would take far longer to complete, but it would not be the end of my book.

Choose Better over Bitter

The church that I had started twenty-three years earlier was gone. For ninety days I walked along the Oregon coast, trying to figure out how to make things right. Amid all this pain and grief, I realized that I still loved what I did. I loved helping people discover their breakthrough moments and build their dreams. Toward the end of my time at the coast, I received an offer from a church in Bellevue, Washington, to conduct their Wednesday night services for the next month. The church was tiny; the drive, six hours round trip.

I responded with an immediate and grateful yes. Two of my closest friends and colleagues from the Living Enrichment Center accompanied me. And the services in Bellevue gave me an idea.

Driving home one night, I asked my friends to help me find a place where we could hold a Tuesday evening service in Portland. Don't get me wrong. I had no intention of starting another church. I knew that was not my path. But I had another debt to pay to our congregants that had nothing to do with money. I had spent more than two decades ministering to so many people: I performed their babies' christenings, conducted their weddings, and buried their parents. We had traveled a journey together, but they never had a chance to question me or to voice their feelings. I knew some of them needed to express their fury; others would want the chance to accuse me, and others still needed support. I told my friends, "I need to let them get mad at me in person. They can accuse me or cry with me, or both. I need to make myself available." My friends and I rented a small space on Tuesday evenings and put the word out about what we called Sabbath Tuesdays.

Following a short service, I would answer questions. The first evening, I looked out at a sea of faces, many of them hostile. I told everyone, "I will stay until all your questions get answered. No questions are out of bounds. Ask me whatever you want." Most of the questions and statements centered on "how could you not know what was happening?" and "you did know, didn't you?" Some people wanted to express their feelings. "You killed our church," one woman said. I couldn't change what had happened. But I could stand in the truth of what had transpired, not holding anything back. People cried and raised their voices; we grieved together. I wanted to do right by these people who had lost their spiritual home. And I wanted to emerge from this entire experience having made a stand for better, not bitter.

In all candor, the first three months were rough. But over time, something shifted, and people showed up for what had become a weekly service, without the need for questions and answers afterward. I had moved to California and would fly up every week to conduct services. This went on for nearly three years.

Although I would never wish what I went through on anyone, I do wish where that journey took me for everyone.

Then came time for the final service. I concluded my talk stating, "We're going to end this the way we started. I will stay until all your questions are answered. Ask me whatever you want." Nearly every hand in the room shot up. A lump of dread rose in my throat. I thought we had put the past behind us. Nervously, I pointed to a woman in the front row. "Mary," she said, "tell us what your children are up to these days." Others asked, "Is your son Rich still acting?" "Is John still living in Mexico?" None of the former parishioners focused on the past; they were excited for my future. What a sweet energy emanating from people I had the privilege of working with all these years. When I walked out of our rented facility that last evening, I felt like the clouds had parted and a moonbeam landed on my forehead, leaving a gold star. My inner voice whispered, "You're free to go."

My friends—Wayne Dyer, Les Brown, Marianne Williamson, and Bob Proctor—encouraged me to build my own coaching business, which I did, while repaying the congregants with every paycheck I received. I didn't have the resources, but I believed in the invisible, invincible laws that connect each one of us. To me, that represents an Infinite source. "I will apply the same transformational system to this task that seems so immense," I thought, "and I will either learn how to do it or die trying." I started paying back the debts in 2005, using the Brave Thinking Tools I was developing. I visualized myself writing the final check and receiving an email that read: "Your debt is now zero."

I wrote that final check in November of 2018. It took more than thirteen years to accomplish a task that at the beginning seemed insurmountable. Had I given in to the temptation to become embittered by loss and shame, I would not have had the spiritual energy for this endeavor. I felt a wave of gratitude for all my study in transformation that had shown me how to apply the reliable, repeatable system of transformation that unlocks the potential in every one of us. Even though I lost what I had built, I still had the awareness that built it—only now I was wiser, having learned from my failure. Although I would never wish what I went through on anyone, I do wish where that journey took me for everyone.

Every one of us has known failure, large or small. Writers draft technical journals while fantasizing about the Pulitzer Prize. Would-be entrepreneurs spend years toiling for others, waiting for the moment to strike out on their own, only to shut down their endeavor. During the COVID pandemic, so many chefs who fulfilled their dream of opening their own restaurant were forced to close them down, many permanently. Failure offers valuable feedback when you take the lessons and use them to guide you forward in your dream-building. Continue to challenge your thinking regarding any perceived failure. Ask yourself, "What is the feedback this 'failure' has for me? Is there another way to perceive the situation that can support my dream, or am I truly being redirected to something greater?" Failure becomes feedback when you take the learning it offers you and use it to guide you forward in your dream-building.

When your dreams are dashed, you can choose to become bitter, or you can choose to become better. The world is full of people who remain shackled to broken dreams, using failure to rationalize staying stuck. We have all known people who remain at a job they despise for twenty-five years or more, complaining bitterly each day and always reminding us, "I could have been... I should have been... I would have been... but I got cheated out of my chance... my promotion... my dream." They are stuck believing life "did it" to them, not detecting the power they possessed all along to cocreate with the Infinite. If you become bitter, your capacity to see future opportunities dies with your failed dream. When you keep feeling sorry for yourself, you cannot grow. You remain stuck, never emboldened to move into a greater dream.

If you know in your heart that you have done everything possible to build a particular dream, and what you have set your heart on does not come to pass, trust that something

BRAVE THINKING TOOL

You are one thought away from transforming a situation into a positive or a negative

better is trying to happen. The Infinite's will is for our greatest good. Our dream is for a particular good. Sometimes we fail because we have not been diligent or persistent enough. Other times we have truly done everything possible and still fall short. Then our challenge is not to stare longingly at a door that is bolted shut but to find the open window where a guiding light beckons. You lean into a new dream, even if you can barely glimpse its outline from where you stand. Move toward the light and lean toward the good.

By choosing better over bitter, Nelson Mandela was awarded the Nobel Peace Prize and became the first Black president of South Africa. As a young man, Mandela was committed to overthrowing the system of apartheid in his country. At first, his protests were peaceful. But after a group of peaceful Black demonstrators was massacred, he began launching militant campaigns to sabotage the government. Following several arrests, he was sentenced to life in prison. His first eighteen years were spent in a brutal prison, where he was confined to a cell without a bed or plumbing. He spent twenty-seven years behind bars before being released in 1990. Four years later, he became president.

For years, I dreamed of someday meeting this great man. After all, who on our planet can become the president of a country that had once sentenced him to life in prison? Only one person—Nelson Mandela. I wondered about the inner process that allowed him to create a life that defied every conceivable circumstance. In 1999, I was invited to speak at the Parliament of the World's Religions, an organization created to foster harmony and engagement to achieve a more just and peaceful world. The meeting was held in Cape Town, South Africa. Upon arriving, I learned I would be part of a six-person private meeting with Mandela. We were instructed not to use flash photography during our time with him. While imprisoned, Mandela had been forced into hard labor in a quartz quarry, and the harsh reflection of the sun had burned his retinas. When he met with our group, Mandela graciously invited any questions we might have. I asked him what it took for someone to become the president of a country that had sentenced him to life in prison.

"The guy who went to prison could never have become president," Mandela told me. "That guy was angry. He was bitter." Referring to his failed efforts to end apartheid, he said all he could think was "it's all lost." And his despair was like a dark cloud over him. Mandela said that over time, however, he learned to climb what he called "the slope of thought" and realized that his being in prison could play a role in ending apartheid. "I had to become pure in my own thinking and move from rage and resentment," he said. With the help of fellow prisoners, Mandela smuggled letters— even his own autobiography—out of prison, helping the anti-apartheid movement stay alive.

Common-Hour Thinking is controlled by logic and circumstances and would predict that someone like Mandela would remain embittered and angry. Instead, he embodied the transformative power of Brave Thinking. Mandela rose above the atrocities that had once embittered him, developing a formidable spirit that advanced the lives of millions of South Africans and became one of the greatest humanitarians of our time.

Tap Into the Power of Forgiveness

The Dalai Lama said, "We can never make peace in the outer world until we make peace with ourselves." To transform the pain of the past, we must begin by forgiving ourselves and others. This work requires Brave Thinking because forgiving someone who has wronged you is not logical. Do you have a story, an authentic grievance? Of course you do. We have all been treated unfairly. We have all been betrayed or diminished by someone's cruelty. You may have every justification for hanging on to your anger and grief. Who can blame you? Still, hanging on takes so much effort. It saps our aliveness, shuts us down, and distances us from our dream. You can't grow a healthy dream in a toxic environment. By staying stuck in bitterness, you block the good that is supposed to be yours.

As you have probably heard, holding on to resentments is like drinking poison and expecting the other person to die. Left to fester, these emotions grow in you like a parasite. Feelings of hatred and resentment stay bottled up inside, seeping into other areas of your life. The offender does not suffer. It is your own dreams that are endangered.

Know this: You do not need to be in that place anymore. Even as we wallow in our resentments, that still, small voice is within us, calling us to higher ground. I know because I am practiced at trying to drown it out with my stories of grievance and justification. If I had stayed with my stories, you would not be reading this book because I would still be in that dark night where I saw myself only as fallen and damaged.

So how do you cleanse yourself of this poison? My clients have told me beautiful stories that echoed my own experience. Some were inspired by the example of great souls like Gandhi or Nelson Mandela. Others were lifted by the words of their spiritual leader or their best friend. And some just got tired of the cycle of feeding and fighting the infection that made them emotionally and spiritually ill. These brave individuals who finally chose to forgive had one thing in common: a moment of humility. When they realized that resentment did not make them superior to the individual they felt had wronged them, they could let go. It is through forgiveness, not resentment, that you will become more powerful. Releasing this feeling allows you to devote energy to building your dream. Forgiveness frees.

And, as Lauren Brollier Newton discovered, forgiveness is ultimately a gift you give yourself.

When I first met Lauren, she was amid what she called a "surprise divorce," since she was still a newlywed. Many wedding gifts were still in their boxes. At night, Lauren's husband moved as far away from her as possible in the bed, pulled the covers over his head, and went to sleep. In the morning, he barely said a word before leaving for work. "I believed I was flawed," she said, "that I needed to be prettier, or thinner, or sexier."

One evening her husband came home from work and announced, "You are not my dream girl." Then he pro-ceeded to list all the qualities that a dream girl would have that she did not. He told her, "You bring nothing to the table." Lauren believed him.

A marriage that had barely begun was ending, but the damages continued to pile up. A few weeks later, Lauren learned her husband had been living a double life with a long-time girlfriend. Lauren felt terribly betrayed. Then one day, when she was at work, her husband moved out, taking their dogs with him. Lauren was crushed that she never had a chance to say goodbye to her beloved pets. She was angry at her husband. "But who I was really angry at was me, because a part of me had always known that he wasn't a good guy, and I didn't listen to myself," she said. "And I was very, very ashamed to be thirty years old and getting a divorce."

A friend of Lauren's invited her to one of my Dream-Builder Live seminars. By that point she was in the middle of her divorce, felt dissatisfied with her work, and was concerned for her health, too. A reading specialist for a school district, she served the community's most underserved children. She loved making a difference in their lives but the hour-long commute each way, her fifty-hour work week, and a discouraging paycheck had worn her out. Lauren had put on an unhealthy amount of weight and developed high blood pressure. She had three goddaughters whom she adored, but whenever they invited her to visit, she turned them down. She was just too busy and exhausted.

Lauren experimented with a Brave Thinking Tool—the question "What would I love?"—envisioning herself three years in the future. Lauren realized she wanted to fall in love again, and she wanted to fulfill her childhood dream of becoming an inspirational speaker. When she was growing up, the other kids watched Sunday morning cartoons while Lauren glued her eyes to ministerial broadcasts. As a child, she didn't care about the religious piece, but she loved how the stories made her feel.

After the seminar, I continued to work with Lauren, and she came to see that if she truly wanted a life she would love in all four quadrants—health and well-being, love and relationships, vocation, and time and money freedom—she had to free herself from the anger and bitterness toward her ex-husband.

What we want most is not vengeance but love. At the most profound and true level, people who have hurt us the most can offer the greatest gifts.

I have forgiveness work to do

The first step toward transforming the pain of the past is an acknowledgment: *I have forgiveness work to do.*

Many budding dream builders have told me that they have no one to forgive, because the person who wronged them does not merit compassion. Characterizing someone as beyond forgiveness lets us off the hook—or so we think. Unfortunately, this position denies us the gift that forgiveness brings. In every person's mind is a place where some resentment or hurt dwells. We like to think we are punishing our enemy by holding a grudge, but every relationship—no matter its current state—is an invitation to experience a more expansive life. There was no denying the cruelty and betrayal of Lauren's ex-husband. But she was also tired of, as she put it, "walking around angry" and rehearsing her hurts. Betrayal contains within it a seed of opportunity. We can choose to reconcile the hurtful experience with what we desire most in life. And what we want most is not vengeance but love. At the most profound and true level, people who have hurt us the most can offer the greatest gifts.

We can learn to open our hearts and find entrance into an everlasting, unconditional love.

This task requires Brave Thinking. To touch this love, you are required to open your heart at the precise moment when every instinct urges you to shut it down. Closing your heart does not build what you want to experience and traps you in the painful feelings, like those Lauren was experiencing.

I can't do it alone

Lauren took the next step to forgiveness, which is a realization: *I can't do it alone.* Lauren learned a meditation to tap into her Infinite source of power, a meditation I learned decades ago at a Human Unity Conference in India. Two hundred religious leaders had the opportunity to meditate and pray with the Dalai Lama, who introduced us to a practice called the loving-kindness meditation. The words are simple yet speak directly to the heart. Some Buddhists repeat the meditation three times a day for twelve weeks to extend loving-kindness to themselves, then out to the world. The following is a portion of this meditation, which I have shared with many of my coaching clients over the years:

> May I be happy. May I be free from suffering. May I be free from tension, fear, worry. May I be at peace.
>
> Just as I wish to be happy, so might you be happy. May you be happy and free from suffering. May your tension, may your painfulness of heart fall away. May your joy increase. May you be free from suffering.
>
> May we all be happy. May we each come into the light. May we let go of the blocks. May we let go of our suffering and experience our perfect being. May we all be free from suffering. May we all be happy.

May all beings be happy. May all beings be clear-minded. May their hearts open. May they be free from suffering.

May all beings be free from suffering. May they love themselves. May they come into their happiness. May they uncover the joy of the true self. All beings everywhere.

At first, Lauren said she didn't want to say those words. But she stayed with the practice. "Every day I would repeat, 'May he truly be happy. May he know peace.'" Along the way, she gained a new awareness. She was grateful to her former husband, because, as she put it, "The most loving thing he ever did was to let me go." She also realized that forgiveness would create space inside her to start turning up the volume on her vision for love. Once you experience the powerful healing inside yourself that forgiveness brings, you begin directing similar energy outward.

Lauren envisioned a man who would be loving and thoughtful, and who would share adventures with her. Within a short time, she did meet her dream man. Today, the two of them are happily married. Lauren's health improved. She spends time with her three goddaughters and has become a successful life coach and speaker, fulfilling her childhood dream.

In you resides a source that is greater than any relationship difficulty. No good comes from rehearsing your hurts. Spirit is inviting you to a new beginning. *A Course in Miracles* asks, "What could you possibly want that forgiveness does not offer?" The answer to that question is "nothing."

I desire a shift

The next step to forgiveness is an affirmation: *I desire a shift.* I have told you about my mentor, the late Jack Boland, a minister and inspirational speaker whose wisdom empowered people from all walks of life to live more abundantly. You might think someone of his standing would never have spent years tormented by a relationship, refusing to forgive his transgressor. Yet that is exactly what happened. We all have forgiveness work to do. Jack could not forgive his former brother-in-law. Not only had he cheated Jack in a business venture, but he also attempted to ruin Jack's impeccable reputation for integrity. This man took every opportunity to make Jack look bad.

"I had a list of grievances a mile long," Jack told me. "Anyone who heard that list could easily jump to my defense, and I was very good at using that story to get people on my side." Jack said he nursed that hurt, cursed it, and rehearsed it for many years. Then one day he thought, "Who is being hurt here? I haven't seen this guy in years, but he lives inside me every day of my life. Who is this hurting? It's hurting *me*!" Jack had withheld his forgiveness because he felt the man didn't deserve a pardon. He deserved punishment.

Jack suddenly realized that forgiveness had nothing to do with his former brother-in-law. He needed to forgive to free his own life. Every prisoner needs a jailer. You think of yourself as the jailer of the person you have condemned without recognizing that, as the guard, you remain stuck in that same prison every day. Jack asked for help in learning how to forgive. After a period of seeking guidance from the Infinite, an idea came to him. All you need is one tiny spark of willingness, and the universe will rush in to support you.

Forgiveness is hard work and an ongoing practice, but the support is always available once you begin the effort.

Jack had asked the Infinite for support, and the idea came to him: to hold the image of his former brother-in-law in his mind and learn to see him through the lens of love and forgiveness.

The Sanskrit word "namaste" is often translated as "the Light in me recognizes and honors the Light in you." That became Jack's spiritual practice. He would create a mental image of the man's face, but instead of seeing him in the light of forgiveness, he just got angry all over again. The more he told himself, "I'm going to think love! I'm going to think love!" the angrier he became.

"Now what?" Jack asked. Again, an idea came to him. Jack recalled the face of his son as a little boy. He immediately felt a surge of love for that child with his sweet gap-toothed smile. Then right in its place, he slipped in the face of his former brother-in-law. His energy of love decreased but not as quickly as before. He practiced diligently for weeks until he could see the man's face in his mind and begin to feel real love, not for what his brother-in-law had done, but for the being that was this man, for the child that he once had been. Another variation on this technique is to look at a childhood photograph of the person who has wronged you and practice imagining your nemesis as an innocent child.

Months later, Jack knew the process had been successful. He was driving to an appointment when a brand-new Cadillac pulled up next to him at a stoplight. He thought, "Wow, that's a nice car." He glanced over and saw that the driver was none other than his former brother-in-law. He immediately thought, "He must be doing well, at least financially. That's nice." In that moment Jack knew his heart had healed. He was free.

We start with acknowledging that we have forgiveness work to do. We recognize that it can't be done alone. We desire to shift to a higher perspective. When we take that step, asking to let go, whatever has kept us in the shadows can no longer pose a threat. What we thought had power over us has none without our permission.

Let me forgive myself

The final step in forgiveness is a request: *let me forgive myself.* Sometimes the biggest grudge we hold is against ourselves. But the universe holds no such grudges. Look closely at your worst moment and see if you can find some good in it. One of the biggest mistakes I ever made was becoming pregnant my junior year in high school. That mistake hurt my parents, got me kicked out of high school, and forced Haven to drop out of college to marry me. That mistake shamed me deeply. I came down with a life-threatening kidney disease. Yet in the night before my surgery, the chaplain introduced me to a whole new way of thinking about the Infinite, and about myself.

Without my mistake, I might have never discovered my power to cocreate with the Infinite and become inspired to study the transformational principles that have helped people throughout the world to manifest their dreams. I might never have stayed in a marriage that produced four amazing children who are the light of my life and who have gone on to make a positive impact on the world in various ways. This tremendous shame, this seemingly unforgivable act, paved the path for a greater life than I could have ever imagined. We all make mistakes that are part of a greater design. Within each mistake is an opportunity to learn a lesson that will bring us to a point of awakening. Today is a new opportunity. Remember, a power that is greater than any relationship difficulty you encounter resides in you.

Forgiving ourselves is an ongoing process that can take years. After the Living Enrichment Center collapsed, I spent my days walking along the beach, broadcasting my grief so loudly that I drowned out my inner voice, the trusted voice of guidance that never berated or shamed me. My road to self-forgiveness began that day on the beach when I could hear that still, small voice once again. It whispered, "Mary, you're still breathing." If we are still breathing, that means we have forgiveness work to do, in my case, starting with myself. Right behind those words, I heard, "Dark chapter. Not your whole book." This message gave me hope that despite the seemingly insurmountable circumstances, I could do right by our congregation. I could honor my commitment to repay the congregants and rebuild a life for myself.

Had I waited until my debt was cleared to forgive myself for my role in the collapse of our church, I would never have been free. I would have been too full of grief and self-loathing to build the kind of life where I could pay off that debt. If we cannot forgive or appreciate ourselves, we cannot draw love or appreciation toward us. We give ourselves grace by understanding that we did the best we could with the awareness we had at the time. The freedom to engage with love and life does not exist on the frequency of guilt, shame, or self-loathing.

Once you remove your resistance through the power of forgiveness, you are free to rediscover the power of love, and to realize that it is and always has been in you. We cannot change the past, but forgiving ourselves for what happened changes everything that can happen from now on. Forgiveness is a process. Give yourself permission to turn the light of forgiveness on the part of you that has been suffering because of a lack of understanding and compassion. Write down your feelings as you send a wave of forgiveness and compassion to the version of you who had the perception that caused you pain. Repeat the forgiveness process as often as it takes, because the more you do, the more it will release and free you for a new beginning. Here are some questions to consider as you embark on this exercise:

- What comes to mind when you ask yourself, "What can I forgive in me today?" Be open to the answer. Nothing is too trivial or too big.

- When you think of that situation, and look at it from a bird's-eye view, what perception or meaning did you give it at the time?

- How can you shift your perception or viewpoint of that situation in your life?

- When you begin to shift it, how does it affect your heart and your energy?

- How do you feel when you find the block and begin to release it with forgiveness?

Remember what Thoreau wrote about making your dreams come true. "If one advances confidently in the direction of his dreams... he will meet with a success unexpected in common hours. He will put some things behind..." Forgiveness is not a pardon produced by a judging or vindictive mind. Forgiveness is not logical. It emerges from a sincere willingness to choose love over condemnation. The grace of forgiveness heals our heart whenever we are truly willing.

TRANSFORMING THE PAIN OF THE PAST

Brave Thinking Tool: You are one thought away from transforming a situation into a positive or a negative
A single, powerful thought can shift your perspective to the positive, even the course of your life; one dark chapter is not your whole book.

Teaching points

- Acknowledge your pain: sit with the darkness without wishing it away, so you can see the good even in the bad, and in time, release your pain.

- Choose better over bitter in the aftermath of failure or loss. Choosing to become bitter keeps you stuck; choosing to become better by learning from the experience opens you to a greater dream.

- Tap into the power of forgiveness; release resentment and you will harness the energy to build your dream.

DESIGNING NEW PARADIGMS

"*There is no planet, sun, or star that could hold you if you but knew who you are.*"

RALPH WALDO EMERSON

Vision-driven thoughts

Can design new paradigms

Repetition works.

DOROTHY GREW UP during the Great Depression. Born in Montana in 1918, she lost her mother at age four. Dorothy had an eighteen-month-old sister and a newborn brother. Her grieving father put his family on a train to Oregon, where his widowed mother lived, so she could help raise the kids. The family barely subsisted on her father's wages, which he earned cutting hair for thirty-five cents a head. Dorothy wore shoes with holes in them. She owned two dresses: one for church and the other she put on for school—five days a week. Students whose families were better off belittled her, an experience that caused her shame she would carry for most of her life.

Dorothy grew up in a home filled with love, and with tremendous loss: of her mother in early childhood; her sister, when Dorothy was sixteen; and her father, who passed away when Dorothy was twenty-three. She was also deeply affected by her family's poverty, which left her insecure and fearful of what people would think of her. Still, she graduated from high school and took a job as a secretary. When she was twenty, she met the man who would become her husband, and a year later they were married.

For much of her early life, Dorothy experienced an abundance of love—from her grandmother, from her father, from her husband—but very little money. Her experience seemed to dictate, "You can have love, but not money." For her, it was an either/or situation; that was her paradigm.

A paradigm is a construct that guides your view of the world and your beliefs about how the world works. Paradigms are the beliefs that you acquire over time. Negative paradigms protect the status quo, the mindset that makes positive changes feel unfamiliar and uncomfortable, and the fears that tell you that if you try, you will fail.

Like any paradigm, Dorothy's belief was born from her circumstances, and once the belief solidified in her, those circumstances repeated. This woman's paradigm deeply affected me because Dorothy was my mother.

Growing up, I knew my mother and father loved each other; they were best friends their entire lives together. But my mother also had a scarcity mentality and was scarred by the girls who bullied her for her shabby clothes. When I was little and asked for something new, I'd be reminded that "money doesn't grow on trees." Playing outside, I was always on my best behavior, heeding my mother's warning: "What would the neighbors think?" As a kid, I accepted the paradigms I was given, just as most of us do, and they became my unconscious thought patterns.

Reimagine Your Life at Any Age

My father developed dementia in his early eighties. When my mother could no longer care for him, we found a wonderful facility close by where we could visit him regularly.

Shortly before his death at age eighty-five, we brought him back home. One day, I entered the house to find my mother huddled in a corner of their bedroom, sobbing. I sat down on the floor and put my arms around her. "I feel like half my body's being cut off," she said. "How will I ever find my way after he's gone?" My parents had been married for sixty-three years.

After my father passed away, my mother fell into a deep depression that lasted six months. Then one day, she called me and said, "I guess if God is still breathing in me, maybe I should try that DreamBuilder thing you do." I couldn't believe it. My mom had been around my work for many years but had never been *in* it. I seized the opportunity, and we began the dream-building process together.

It took baby steps for the both of us. I didn't start by asking her what her dream life would look like. After all, she was still deeply grieving the life she had lost with my father. She wasn't ready for anything dramatic, but I knew she had longing in her, some dissatisfaction that she was trying to scratch. I asked her if there was a hobby that interested her, perhaps something that had excited her at one time. I was looking for the sprouts of a new life that might want to emerge. She told me that about twenty years earlier, she had wanted to take classes in painting porcelain china but hadn't pursued the idea. "I might learn to paint," she said now.

Hers was a modest dream, but that was all we needed: a glimmer of an unlived life, some small desire that we could surface. My mother was practicing Brave Thinking by stating a desire without worrying how she would proceed. Together, we looked for painting classes and she quickly became a star student. In her eighties, my mother discovered that she was a talented artist. Over the next five years, she gave her beautifully painted plates, bowls, and vases as gifts, signed with her name. After some of her pieces were displayed in a Portland gallery, word got out, leading to a one-woman show in galleries throughout the Pacific Northwest.

For her ninetieth birthday, she wanted to celebrate in a bold way. She had attended lectures, including one by Muhammad Yunus, who founded the Grameen Bank and was also a microfinance pioneer. His talk captured my mother's imagination. She decided to start a nonprofit organization that granted microloans to people whose spouses had been injured or killed in the Iraq or Afghanistan wars. My father had done two tours of duty, first in World War II, and then in Korea. He had been overseas for a total of three and half years, while my mother worked and took care of my older sister. During his second tour, she had two daughters to care for. She remembered her struggle and wanted to help families that carried even greater burdens. To raise funds for her nonprofit, she wrote a book, *Put a Zip in Your Day!*, a collection of ninety ideas to make each day more enlivening.

Following this, my mom decided to attend one of the women's retreats I had been hosting for nearly thirty years. She especially enjoyed a tradition called the Wise Women's Council that brought the elders in our audience to the stage to share their wisdom and respond to questions, none of which were out of bounds. This time the women—the youngest being in her mid-eighties—spoke about sex, dating, and their ongoing work and hobbies. Someone asked my ninety-two-year-old mother if she'd thought about remarrying. "I don't want to be anybody's nursemaid," she said, "but if there was somebody interesting who wanted to go to lectures, movies, or plays, or watch sports, it would be fun to have a companion."

Life is no respecter of age. As long as you are breathing, the universe keeps sending you signals to live fully. But if your paradigm is "I'm too old and my time is past," you might keep breathing, but the quality of your life diminishes. You'll just be waiting, but for what?

My mother was bursting with possibilities that night at the retreat. We didn't know that by the following weekend she would be gone.

Mom had come to stay with me for a week, in anticipation of Mother's Day the following Sunday. That Wednesday she had a massive heart attack. Her choice was either open-heart surgery or do nothing and slip away in the next twenty-four to forty-eight hours. She asked for twenty minutes to get quiet and decide her path.

My mother chose to slip away. She called her loved ones. Grandchildren arrived to be with her. On Friday she told me, "If I can get out of here by tomorrow, then I won't have died on Mother's Day." Who thinks this up? A woman who knows what it is like to grow up without a mother. I had mine for sixty years.

"I feel like I'm complete," she told me. True to her word, she passed away at 11:37 p.m.

In the last years of her life, my mother became an artist and author, she started a nonprofit organization helping others, and acted as an elder and mentor to many. Her most creative years were between the ages of eighty-five and ninety-two. She lived a full, rich life, dreaming till the very end. Despite growing up with incredible hardship and having every reason to stick to her old paradigms, my mother showed me how quickly a person can reinvent herself.

A few years later, I was speaking in Seattle. After my presentation, an older couple approached me. "We have your mother to thank for our new dining room table," the husband said. I thought, "What is he talking about?" The husband explained, "We bought *Put a Zip in Your Day!* and we decided we're going to do every one of her ninety tips, and that included buying a new dining table." That was Dorothy.

Wherever you are and whatever the qualifiers you hold— I'm too old, I'm too young, when I lose weight, when I gain weight, when I retire, when the kids are grown—please know that life is not waiting for that perfect moment.

Someday, we will put our heads on our pillows for the last time. We don't know when that day will come. Most of us do not get ninety-two years. But whatever time we have, I hope we can learn from the example of Dorothy and realize that it is never too late to reimagine your life or change the way you see the world.

A paradigm is a collection of assumptions and theories that determine how we see the world and ourselves in it. Paradigms provide a context from which you operate every day, including how you perceive your well-being, interact with others, approach work, and spend time. In other words, your paradigms influence all four quadrants of your life: health and well-being, love and relationships, vocation, and time and money freedom. So deeply ingrained do they become in our psyche that even when we are presented with information that directly contradicts our paradigm, we ignore or explain away that data, allowing an unhealthy paradigm to diminish our dream. That's where the Brave Thinking Tool "Begin with the end in mind" comes in. For your dreams to manifest, you need to focus on the result you desire. Continue your practice of imagining yourself

BRAVE THINKING TOOL

Begin with the
end in mind

living in the future as if it has already happened. Revisit your vision statement. In this new life you have described so vividly, does your framework for viewing the world still fit? Through increasing your awareness and focus, you can change your paradigms to align with your vision.

When I got my first Apple computer many years ago, its operating system was called Panther. It provided a certain amount of access and different things I could do. When I installed the next level of operating system, Tiger, and then Leopard, the capability expanded greatly. The equipment hadn't changed, but the operating system had. This is a clue for you. With your Brave Thinking skills, you are changing your life's operating system. You can't just get rid of the old one. You must replace an outdated system with a new one.

Keep in mind: your operating system isn't inherently good or bad. Your current computer's operating system seems fine because you are accustomed to the way it functions. Similarly, your internal operating system feels "normal" to you. It uses your voice, sounds like you, and behaves like you. You might even be seduced into believing that it is the totality of you when, in fact, it is outmoded mind-ware. An old operating system is an analogy for your old paradigm. But unlike the straightforward process of upgrading from Panther to Tiger, your old paradigm will fight like a lion rather than be upgraded. It will argue for delay and bring on distraction and dissuasion. It will attack you relentlessly with fear and shame. You will feel like you've done something wrong—but your discomfort is a sign of your growth. This chapter will prepare you for the struggle that comes with the upgrade that will give you the power to think bravely and live the life you love.

There's a Hindu story about a traveler who comes across an aged wise man sitting on a curb just outside a small town. He stops and asks, "Wise man, tell me, what kind of people are in this village?"

The elderly man responds, "Tell me of the people who dwell in the village from which you came."

The newcomer sits down, scrunches up his face, and lets out a litany of complaints. "Oh, they were horrible: mean, nasty, and self-centered. They were always thinking about themselves."

The wise man says, "You know, those are exactly the same kind of people who live in this village." Upon hearing this bad news, the visitor quickly gathers his belongings and sets off in search of friendlier territory.

Not long after, another traveler approaches the edge of town and encounters the same wise man.

"Tell me," he asks, "what kind of people live in this village?"

The older fellow gives him the identical response: "Tell me of the people who dwell in the village from which you came."

"Wonderful people," the traveler replies. "They are kind, generous, the most considerate people you could imagine."

"Those are exactly the kind of people who live in this village," the wise man assures him.

We create the "kind of people" in our lives through our paradigms. If our perspective is that people are fundamentally untrustworthy, we interpret their behavior as such. Those who reach out their hand to us are not giving but grabbing. Whatever image your mind clings to tends to replicate itself in your real world.

A woman I know, Kaitlyn, who had been painfully hurt over past rejections, finally met the man of her dreams. One evening, he brought her home earlier than she expected, explaining that he had a major deadline at work. "I won't be able to see you this week," he said. Given how much time the two of them had been spending together, the message Kaitlyn heard was, "I'm dumping you. I'm nicer than the other guys you've dated, so I'm rejecting you in a classy way, but either way, we're through." He started to say something about calling her every night, but Kaitlyn tuned him out, practically slamming the door in his face.

She saw what she believed to be true, that any man who got to know her would eventually leave. The poor fellow went home and, for the first time, had second thoughts about the relationship, just as Kaitlyn had predicted. Was Kaitlyn justified in her suspicions? Or was she amiss for jumping to the wrong conclusion? It does not matter. We respond to what we perceive as the truth, based on our paradigms. Kaitlyn's paradigm told her that she was unlovable.

Believing in a self-defeating paradigm crushes our dreams, again and again. Unless Kaitlyn learns to recognize herself as lovable, she will always pull too hard on others, wanting them to fill a hole in her heart. When I see myself as unacceptable, I will create an experience that validates my belief.

In a scene in the rom-com classic *Sleepless in Seattle*, Annie (played by Meg Ryan) is a single woman, a journalist, who becomes incensed when a coworker repeats the popularly reported statistic that shot fear into America's population of single women in real life: that women over forty were more likely to be killed by a terrorist than to get married. Annie points out that this statistic had turned out to be untrue, to which her editor, played by Rosie O'Donnell, quips that it *feels true*.

If it "feels true" that your partner will dump you, like Kaitlyn, you will seek out a dumpster with your name on it at every corner. Remind yourself to begin with the end in mind, what you truly desire, and look closer at the "facts" that block your path. Try to remember that the "facts" of your life carry no more weight than the meaning you attach to them. Facts change and can be examined from alternate angles and possess no more power over us than the credence we give them. If we believe they are powerful enough to stop us, they halt our progress. If we look higher, to the Infinite, we begin to attract opportunities, ideas, and people in harmony with that mental attitude. Our paradigm shifts.

No matter how readily you believe that thoughts pop into your head of their own accord, you choose what takes up space in your mind.

Here is a practice that I find helpful: *seek a second opinion*. Whenever you find yourself disappointed, stuck, or rejected, remember that a more expansive perspective is always available. No matter how readily you believe that thoughts pop into your head of their own accord, you choose what takes up space in your mind.

Often a second opinion is warranted. Pause and ask for one from the Infinite. Consulting your Higher Power allows you to lift your own thoughts to a higher perspective and believe the best about yourself or someone else. This practice removes the filter that distorts reality and allows every positive intention to shine through.

Paradigms are not ultimately real or true. They are a model for the world that help you navigate more efficiently, relieving you of the overhead of constant executive decisions. They hold you back when you find yourself living under new circumstances but still operating under old beliefs. Some paradigms are limiting, others are expansive. For example:

- "Nothing ever goes right for me" versus "I'm a person for whom things work out."

- "I'm a woman over fifty, and all the good ones are taken" versus "I'm a woman in her prime, and my soulmate awaits me."

- "It's too late to start over" versus "the best is yet to come."

When you shift your paradigm, everything changes. A paradigm is a pattern of thinking that produces a pattern of being that generates a pattern of results. If you took a piece of paper and put iron filings on it, then placed an electromagnet underneath, those iron filings would subtly move into the pattern that is congruent with a magnetic field. Although you cannot see this magnetic field, it exists. If you amplify the current in the electromagnet, the filings will snap into place more quickly and with more force and staying power. That is what Brave Thinking does. It brings new power to the pattern that is congruent with your vision.

If you want to know what the pattern produces, look at your results. They are a perfect reflection.

Many years ago, I worked with a woman in our congregation whose dream was for a loving relationship with her sons, but her paradigm was "mother knows best." She loved her boys dearly, but she also had precise expectations of their behavior. Ever since they were little, whenever they failed to do as she expected, she would point out their faults. They would sulk or snap back, and another argument would ensue. The pattern of struggle was so deeply ingrained, it felt almost inevitable. One summer, the youngest son—now a grown man—scheduled a vacation to see his mother after a year-and-a-half absence. When he arrived, her mouth dropped open. Her clean-cut baby had turned into an unshaven mess. His hair, streaked blue, was long enough for a ponytail. His clothes looked like thrift-store rejects. She was ready to pounce, thinking, "This isn't how I raised you. You look like a criminal."

She stopped herself just in time. During the past year, she had been working on getting closer to God and had come to recognize both her paradigm and her own capacity to create a different relationship with her children. She asked for the Infinite's help in forging that relationship. As she did so, she heard the words, "Does your son have to look a certain way for you to love him?"

"But the blue hair!" she replied instantly, before asking herself: "What do I want more? To be right about my son's hair or to have a relationship with him?" She sat down and listened to his stories about work and friends and never once criticized his appearance. It was a glorious visit and she learned more about her son that week than she had in the past decade.

We can seek support in replacing unhealthy paradigms with empowering ones. Consider asking a trusted loved one to be candid about a pattern that may be causing some distance, and then write down each time you catch yourself in that behavior.

Many years ago, I asked my adult children this question, and every one of them answered identically: The cell phone! "Mom, your phone interrupts our visits and we end up feeling less important than your work," my daughter, Jennifer, told me. I was sure my kids had exaggerated my phone time, until I jotted down every call that came in when I was with them and the length of time that those calls pulled me away from their company. *Ouch*! I was appalled by how I had allowed work to intrude on my sacred time with family.

Like my mother, I had a paradigm that produced scarcity thinking: "I'm responsible for the income that supports my family. If I don't answer these calls right now, it will put my business at risk." I didn't believe I could have both a thriving business *and* the time I wanted with my family. By asking my children for their candor, I recognized my pattern and shifted that to an empowering paradigm instead: "There is plenty of time for me to have uninterrupted time with family and build a thriving business helping everyone I want to help." By telling myself that repeatedly, I began to see evidence of its truth. I learned to push the "off" button on my cell phone, giving the "on" signal to my loved ones.

When you work with your paradigm, remember that a part of you wants to move forward and another part of you wants to maintain your current reality. Navigating change always involves a choice—"will I or won't I take the next step?" Your paradigm speaks to you when you grow. It stays mute only when you remain safely within your comfort zone. If you don't feel the least bit of fear or doubt, either your dream is not big enough or you are not in touch with your vision. The key to understanding your paradigm is to notice when you feel resistance to something new. Discomfort and doubt emerge at a crucial moment to warn you that your old paradigm has resurfaced, and that now is your opportunity to repattern your thoughts.

For example, an offer for a job with increased responsibility will take you out of your comfort zone and you might feel uneasy. You can bring awareness to your discomfort and tell yourself, "I know this is a risk and it makes me anxious, but I'm ready for the challenges. I am skilled and I can handle it." You are now beginning to reprogram your paradigm by acknowledging your worries and moving forward anyway. The allure of the familiar is strong; overcoming its pull requires significant mental energy. Repatterning your thoughts is no small task, so what can you do? Should you just white-knuckle through it? Or does an easier strategy exist?

Overcoming procrastination, excuses, and doubt

Did you know that more than 90 percent of the fuel in the space shuttle boosters was used to raise it to only 5 percent of its final orbital altitude? In much the same way, you need the most energy to overcome the "gravitational pull" of the familiar in your life when you are just getting started. Your paradigm is the strong force that causes you to make excuses, procrastinate, and say that your dream can't come true. Surprisingly, your paradigm is the strongest force that stands in the way of your dream.

When encountering a formidable problem like an entrenched paradigm, try breaking it into smaller pieces that you can address individually. To this end, here are what I call the three Ds of paradigm shifts: distraction, dissuasion, and DEFCON 1.

Defy the Three Ds

You can resist the three D paradigm traps by understanding how they function in you and by using strategies and tactics to prevail against them.

Distraction

Distraction is the sneaky force that keeps you operating in the way you always have. You can have the greatest intention to employ the Brave Thinking Tools and then turn around and six months have gone by. Your old paradigm is winning because the pull toward the familiar is that powerful. Your old paradigm will not bust through the doors of your mind yelling, "Stop taking steps toward your dream!" Distraction is subtler than that. It will sound more like this: "Listen, you have a meeting first thing in the morning on Monday, so you should think about that right now." Or you may hear, "You'll be more creative if you do your laundry and clear your desk first." Your appetite may speak up: "You'll be able to build your dream better if you're not hungry. How about some lunch now?" Or your curiosity will whisper, "You haven't checked your phone in ten minutes. Maybe there's an important message you should read first."

You already have the tools to face these or any other distraction. Because you have practiced noticing your thoughts, you know that at this moment you have reached a crossroads and must decide where you will put your attention. You have a vividly imagined dream of what you would love. This is a good time to pull out "up until now..." Tell yourself, "Up until now I have been distracted by food or Facebook." Can you feel the power of that? I can and I do. I use "up until now" regularly to steer myself from distraction and toward my dream. It has worked for millions and will work for you.

Dissuasion

Your old paradigm is tenacious. If it cannot distract you, then it will come at you with a different tactic. Often your paradigm will protect itself with dissuasion. You may find yourself thinking, "I actually don't want this dream." Think back to the last time you set a big goal for yourself, something that took time and effort to accomplish. Let's say you wanted to be promoted in your job. You planned to set up a meeting with your boss to discuss future opportunities, but before the call, you thought, "I'm busy enough as it is. I don't want the added stress. The raise in pay won't make that much of a difference. I should wait until the kids graduate. What if I get turned down? Maybe I don't want that promotion after all." Dissuasion can be difficult to identify. Even as it steers you away from your dream, your decision seems to make sense because dissuasion comes in the form of your own voice.

But you already have the tools to conquer dissuasion. First, notice statements such as:

- I will always be like this.

- It is so hard.

- I have never been able to...

- I can't.

And you know what to do: You can quickly repattern each of these sentences with "up until now." My son Rich explains how he was under dissuasion's spell and what broke it:

When I was nine years old, I watched *Star Wars* in the theater thirty-eight times. Seeing Luke fly that X-wing starfighter got into my blood. Standing in the fields of the farm where I grew up, I loved to watch the jetliners make white stripes across the sky, amazed that the people on that aircraft were going five hundred miles an hour. I thought, "That's awesome! I want to go five hundred miles an hour." I was fascinated that with the right amount of lift and thrust, drag and weight, an aircraft could lift tons of metal and cargo and people into the air.

I got into college and then life happened: business school, a career in acting, marriage, and children. The story I told myself as I watched airplanes take off and attended air shows was the sad pilot story: "Oh, that would be fun." Although I had my own businesses and could create a schedule for myself, I had become addicted to the story of "oh yeah, that's not something normal people do, and I'm just a normal guy." That was where the story ended for me. "I would love that, but it's just not realistic."

Despite growing up in a family where transformation and dream-building were standard topics of dinner conversation, I was just this sad, grumpy pilot inside who didn't think I could have what I wanted.

Then I had kids. My son's first word, I swear, was "airplane."

After work, I would take him out in front of my house, my son on my hip. He was about ten months old, and he would watch the air traffic at about ten thousand feet above Santa Monica. His eyes would always track the airplanes. And he would point. And every day, I would say, "Yeah, Braden, that's an airplane." And he pointed for weeks and weeks and weeks. And one day he said, "A-pane." And I said, "Honey! He spoke!"

And my wife ran out. "Oh, did he say 'mama'?"

I said, "No."

"Did he say 'dada'?"

"No, he said 'airplane.'"

Right then, Braden said it again: "A-pane." And it never stopped. This aviation enthusiast in our family only grew more passionate. This kid loved anything to do with airports and airplanes.

One day, when he was eight years old, the two of us were in the car and saw a small aircraft flying over Santa Monica Airport, and he said, "Yeah, it's too bad you can't get your pilot's license, Dad, because then we could fly."

I only half heard him, but I immediately responded, "What are you talking about? I can get my pilot's license whenever I want."

The look on that eight-year-old's face when I said those words stopped everything for me. He asked, "Then why *don't* you get your pilot's license?" He assumed I couldn't get a license. Otherwise, why wasn't I flying? That "why" changed my story.

We tell ourselves stories. We tell other people stories. They're usually the same stories. And because I decided to tell a different story, I went from a person who dreamed of flying airplanes to spending ten hours a week for the next six months getting my pilot's license.

Flying has been such a bonding experience for our family. My son also dreams of becoming a pilot. When he was fifteen years old, he'd already had his first six hours of ground school and his first six hours of flight training with an instructor at Palomar Airport in San Diego. During the sixth lesson I was standing on the tarmac watching. In these early lessons, the instructor does the takeoff and landing and the student takes the controls in between. After the plane landed, the instructor ran up to me with Braden in tow. "Mr. Boggs, I've had about four thousand hours of instructing, only twice in those four thousand hours have I had a beginning student do what your son just did. He just landed the plane, unassisted." Unassisted! Do you think I'm glad I changed my story? Real glad.

At eight years old, Braden asked his father, "Then why *don't* you get your pilot's license?" This simple question helped Rich break free of his paradigm and move confidently toward his dream. Braden, now in his early twenties, is close to achieving his dream of becoming a pilot, as well.

DEFCON 1

You're going to feel an uncontrollable or irrational fear that, unchecked, could stop you dead in your tracks when you're building your dream. "DEFCON" is a U.S. military term that stands for "defense readiness condition" and the number 1 is the highest state of alertness in times of national security threats. When you're in a state of DEFCON 1, you have moved past your rational, intellectual thinking. You might begin to feel flushed, jittery, or panicked, and not know why.

I shared my son Mat's story about his kamikaze moment during a football game. He was encountering DEFCON 1. It works like this: A good idea comes to you and you know how to act on it. And yet, the thought of taking that action feels practically life-threatening. In reality, the only life being threatened is the paradigm's life. But this feeling goes right past your logical centers to stimulate the amygdala in the reptilian brain. You feel that rush of fear.

When you recognize DEFCON 1, the paradigm will start to die. It will no longer rule your life with limitations. The challenge is that your paradigm knows *everything* about you. It knows all the times you didn't do what you said you were going to do. It can access the whole filing cabinet of failed attempts, forgotten dreams, and parade of unrealized goals. If your paradigm cannot stop you by distraction or dissuasion, it will try one last strategy: triggering DEFCON 1, your fight-or-flight reflex, which inhibits your ability to confidently apply the right tool to establish a new paradigm.

In this case, before you go to noticing and "up until now," you need to "hit the pause button." That is easy to remember because in the middle of a panic what could be better? Unlike an actual defense emergency, you can hit your internal pause button, take a deep breath to relax, and allow tension to melt away. Now you can call up your dream, use "up until now" and defeat the last of the three *D*s.

Change Your Paradigm, Change Your Life

One of my favorite stories that demonstrates the power of paradigm is about an old man who was fishing off a dock, reeling in one fish after another. Next to him stood a bucket and a ruler that was snapped off at the ten-inch mark. The fisherman would throw out his line and every so often, he'd reel in a little fish. Then he would carefully unhook his catch and lay it down alongside his ruler. He would toss any fish measuring eight or nine inches into his bucket. Pretty soon, there was a big tug on the line. The old guy fought hard with the fish and finally reeled in a beauty. It must have been over a foot long. He placed it alongside his ten-inch ruler, then promptly threw his fish back in the water.

A young man who was new to fishing had been watching the other fellow for hours. Did the older fellow know something he didn't? Maybe there was an ordinance against catching bigger fish? Overcome with curiosity, he broke the silence. "Gosh, I've been watching you all afternoon, and that was the biggest fish you caught so far. It was a beauty. I don't get it. Why did you throw it back?"

The old man looked up at him and shrugged, "I've only got a ten-inch frying pan."

Our frying pan is the size of the life we know. The Infinite sends us fish, ideas, to nourish us, to build our dreams. When it sends an idea that is bigger than the frying pan, we discard it. We throw it back into the sea of ideas, saying,

"No, that that won't fit." Our paradigms tell us we don't have the time, the money, or the wherewithal. You can allow an idea into your life, even if you do not know how to achieve it. The Infinite's currency is ideas. The people who realize their dreams are the ones who are careful not to discard the ideas that can nourish them and lead them to a more abundant life. They realize their frying pan does not span a mere ten inches; rather, its breadth is infinite. When an inspired idea comes your way, let it nourish you.

When I met Jubril Wilson, he was so locked in limited beliefs about himself that there was no room for new ideas, inspired or otherwise. He told me, "Mary, I feel like a loser."

How Jubril felt was not the truth about himself but merely a paradigm that kept him stuck. In fact, Jubril was at his breaking point, struggling just to get by.

A doctor told Jubril he had only two years to live. He had high blood pressure, type 2 diabetes, and fat on his heart. He was going through a messy divorce that had him in and out of court. He felt he had disappointed his mother and daughter. Although he loved his work as a real estate agent, he treated it more like a hobby, earning at most $15,000 a year. He was in a prison of paradigms that had him believing, "You're not a good father. You are a loser with a fat broken heart!"

Jubril felt like he was dying. "I was breathing," he said, "but I wasn't really living." Then a colleague invited him to attend one of my seminars, where he felt such warmth and acceptance, he realized that he wanted—and deserved—a better life. We began working together. Jubril's paradigms shifted when he asked himself for the first time, "What would I love?" He recognized that whatever he focused on expanded. Instead of dwelling on his sadness and self-loathing, he envisioned his life as successful in work, health, and love. In fact, he had an inspiring idea—that I would officiate his marriage to the woman of his dreams.

At the time, however, Jubril was not engaged. He wasn't even dating.

But a year later, I was honored to perform his wedding ceremony to Takisha, truly the woman he had envisioned.

If you focus on what you would love, "it's contagious," he said. "Others see it, believe it, and that love spreads throughout the world. And you attract people you love to be around." Jubril conquered the habit of continually recycling the thoughts that caused him pain. Within six months, he went from earning $15,000 a year to becoming a top agent in his office, earning over $130,000 a year. The financial abundance that Jubril attracted finally allowed him to create the life he had envisioned. He sent his daughter to private school, and as of this writing, she is in college pursuing a degree in engineering.

Jubril became a broker and is now licensed in four states. He donates his time to help aspiring agents and brokers to pass their real estate exams. "Before I didn't see myself as someone who could help others, and now it's my new normal," he said.

Like all of us, Jubril still has paradigms that get him stuck now and then. For him, it's procrastination, for example, being two weeks into a one-month goal with little or no progress. He addresses these struggles by reliving a past triumph—how it felt, what he accomplished, and who he became in the process. Jubril proudly calls himself a Brave Thinker for life. By demonstrating the courage to challenge paradigms that were taking life from him, Jubril said he has realized dreams he couldn't ever have imagined.

Interrupting the broadcast

One of the things I enjoy most about my work is the opportunity to support people like Jubril to recognize their own capacity for transformation. I also love when my friends and clients share strategies they have discovered that further their journey. The late Karen Joyce, a board member at our former church, was one of those individuals. Several years ago, Karen decided to move from Oregon back to her home state of California to pursue her dream of living in the Malibu Hills overlooking the ocean, where she planned to further her career in coaching and teaching.

Karen soon found the perfect house to rent: two stories, with four bedrooms, including a master suite that looked over a gorgeous green backyard. She had an office, plenty of room for guests, and couldn't be happier. A week after she moved in, she called and told me about something strange that had happened.

She had been out for her morning run, when the thought had suddenly struck her, "Maybe you shouldn't have gotten that big house." The thought continued. "You're paying $1,000 a month more than you could be paying. How often are your sons realistically going to visit? They probably won't visit you at the same time anyway, so why do you need three guest rooms? You're wasting $12,000 a year on rent that you could have put toward a down payment. You might as well be flushing money down the toilet." Where had these thoughts come from? Karen wondered.

She stopped running, stomped her foot, and said out aloud, "Excuse me. I interrupt this broadcast with an important message from my soul. I am a child of God and I deserve to live a life I love living." She had never taken that kind of control over her own mind before, and what happened next astonished her. That needling voice went silent.

Our minds continually feed us all kinds of paradigms, voices from the past, and emotions that may no longer serve us. Few people take the time to stop and wonder if they even need to listen to this disempowering prattle.

The truth is you can tell your mind to be quiet. You can interrupt the flood of emotions and speak your truth. You may have to mentally repeat yourself, or like Karen, make an announcement that interrupts the broadcast, but with practice and persistence you can quiet the doubts that try to sabotage your dream. I have mentioned that Buddhists call the chattering mind a "jumping monkey," something that must be tamed. When a thought enters your awareness, you do not have to flatter it with your attention. You can tell it what you're going to think, rather than letting any old thought come at you, or you can simply allow thoughts to come and go chaotically. When an old story or disempowering paradigm pops up, remember that you are the one in control. You can speak to that voice of fear or doubt, addressing it directly.

In this space between dreaming and building, you can double down on the practices that brought you this far. Being a Brave Thinker means holding the impossible in your mind, especially when the old paradigms want to hold you back. We are all meant to feel the incredible power of pushing through an obstacle to reach the other side. You have the ability to let go of old paradigms and replace them with an empowering worldview.

EXERCISE: Truth in Paradigms

Write the words "Present Paradigms" on a piece of blank paper and the word "Truths" on another. On the first piece of paper, write down the negative paradigms that pervade your thinking and interfere with your dream. This paradigm may sound like "people are out to get me" or "you're not good enough" or "now is not a good time" or "you don't have what it takes" or "you've been a fool before, and you're going to be a fool again." Whatever you hear most often, write it down. You may recognize this voice as that of your mother or father, a former partner or spouse, the employer who fired you, or the bully who tormented you at school. Or it may be your own voice that gets in the way of your dream-building.

These paradigms are not real. Your belief gave them life and Common-Hour Thinking nourished them. Those negative beliefs then became real and they have produced your current results. You are more than this, though, more than these voices and more than these results. Your life right now has come from your pattern of thinking before you knew how to be more aware and how to think bravely. There's nothing to be ashamed of, just aware. If you don't counter your paradigms, they will continue wiring and firing inside your brain and keep creating the life you have now.

If you want a different experience, you can generate your truth and let it resonate within your being. What is the truth? You are connected to a power greater than the problem you're facing; therefore, you can tackle any adversity. That's my truth; yours will be specific to you.

Come up with a few truthful statements and write them on your "Truths" paper. This may be as simple as "I have what it takes right now" or "my self-worth doesn't come from the scale." You are so much more than your condition, situation, or even your fear. Channel the part of you that wants to move forward and continue to expand. From that place, write down what is true.

After writing three paradigms and three truths, place the two pieces of paper on the ground in front of you, next to each other. Set a timer for one minute and stand on your "Present Paradigms" paper.

For sixty seconds, speak these paradigms. Say them aloud, every nasty and mean thing your paradigm sparks to the surface when it controls your thoughts. But as soon as that timer goes off, say the words you learned earlier:

Excuse me! I interrupt this broadcast with an important message from my soul. I have a birthright. I deserve to live a life I love living, while I'm living it.

Now, step onto your "Truths" paper and speak your truth for sixty seconds. This can be anything from "I am worth a million dollars a year" to "I deserve an epic love story" or whatever feels good and true to you. Believe it, let it soak out of you and into the Infinite. Speak the truth of the life you would love. By doing this, you are interrupting, releasing, and repatterning your paradigms. Here is a saying worth committing to memory:

I am a luminous light being; there is power in me beyond measure, and I have been given a wonderful dream. I deserve to live a life I love. The Infinite is sending me signals of a greater experience, one designed to make me feel more alive and more connected to everything. I have access to everything required to create my dream. I am connected to a power that knows all things, which I can tap into at any moment. There is always another step I can take, always another form of expansion, a future evolution. I am more than I appear. I always have been, and I always will be.

Most people spend more time planning a vacation than they do looking at, designing, and deciding on a life they would love. That is why it is so important that you have looked at your life, that you noticed your discontent, and that you are now working toward building a better life. People are not afraid of dying; they are afraid of getting to the end of life only to realize they never truly lived. One hospital studied one hundred elderly people facing death and asked them to reflect on their biggest regret. Nearly all of them said they regretted not the things they did but the things they didn't do, the risks they never took, the dreams they never pursued.

Jonas Salk, who developed one of the first successful polio vaccines, didn't earn money from or even patent his discovery because he wanted it to be distributed to as many people as possible. He lived by his own motto: "Hope lies in dreams, in imagination, and in the courage of those who dare to make dreams into reality."

DESIGNING NEW PARADIGMS

Brave Thinking Tool: Begin with the end in mind
Change your paradigms to align with the end result—the manifestation of your vision.

Teaching points
- Reimagine your life at any age, changing the paradigm that you are too old or too young to achieve your dreams.

- Defy the three Ds, namely distraction, dissuasion, and DEFCON 1, by using techniques such as "up until now..." and "hit the pause button."

- Change your paradigm, change your life. When a paradigm is undermining you, shut it down by "interrupting the broadcast" and replacing it with an empowering thought.

Exercise
- Write down your predominant negative paradigm and state it aloud. Recognize that you are more than this limiting belief and have the power to change it. Remind yourself: "I am a luminous light being; there is power in me beyond measure, and I have been given a wonderful dream. I deserve to live a life I love."

PART III

BUILDING

NOW THAT YOU have a blueprint for a life you would love and the necessary tools for bridging the gap between where you are and where you want to be, it is time to act. In part I, "Blueprinting," you brought your longing and discontent to the surface, asking yourself, "What would I love?" In part II, "Bridging," you systematically and scientifically nurtured your dream with more Brave Thinking, befriending fear, deepening your commitment, growing from failure, and releasing the negative paradigms that stood between you and your dream. Now, you are ready to act.

Most people who have a big dream get stuck right out of the gate with the "how." "How am I going to do this? How can this happen? How?" So far in this book, we've held off on the how so that you can clarify the "what," imagining a life you would love so vividly that you see yourself in the future as if it is happening right now. Now that the vision is clear and you have shifted your paradigms to embrace that vision, you are ready to take on the how.

Let's say you are a basketball player, and your dream is to become an excellent free throw shooter. "Building" is game time! Imagine as you are given the ball to take a free throw, both teams are lined up at the edge of the key and the crowd is watching. Your Brave Thinking has brought you to this moment. In your blueprinting work, you let go of self-doubt and limitations and envisioned yourself living in the dream. You imprinted your brave vision in your mind by vividly imagining yourself successfully sinking your free throws. In "Bridging," you practiced science-based techniques to confront fear, change unhealthy paradigms, and focus on your vision. Shot after shot, in the early mornings and late into the night, you worked to make your vision real. You have defined a brave dream, befriended your fears, learned from past failure, and focused on what matters most. Now it is building time, when you bravely act. You are ready. You step up to the line and shoot.

9

FORTIFYING YOUR DREAM

"There are only two ways to live your life.
One is as though nothing is a miracle.
The other is as though everything is a miracle."

ALBERT EINSTEIN

———————

Take a baby step,

Or you can take a huge leap,

But don't just sit there.

———————

P ARDON IF THIS seems nosy, but I'd like to ask you a personal question: What is your first thought as you awaken each morning? Perhaps you immediately recoil, thinking about the day's overwhelming schedule that makes you want to pull the covers over your head and hide. Maybe you ask yourself, "Is that fresh coffee I smell?" and hop out of bed.

My fellow Brave Thinkers, I'd like to share with you a practice I developed more than two decades ago that changed not only the way I start my morning but has brought fulfillment to all four quadrants of my life, to my health and well-being, love and relationships, vocation, and time and money freedom. That practice is gratitude.

Religions and belief systems worldwide emphasize gratitude, one of the oldest spiritual practices on the planet. Gratitude is key to creating a happy, fulfilling, impactful life. Living in a state of gratitude affects your ability to make decisions that propel you forward and, as Thoreau wrote, advance confidently in the direction of your dreams. Practicing gratitude fortifies your dreams, drawing even greater good to you, because gratitude is harmonious with abundance.

But we don't always wake up feeling positive or grateful, especially if we didn't sleep well, the pesky alarm woke us up, or we are troubled and anxious over a difficulty, large or small. How do you get into the habit of living with gratitude? That was my question a couple of decades ago. I developed a simple thirty-second meditative practice that I use each day to generate a state of gratitude.

When I am waking up—whether because of the alarm going off, the sunlight shining on my face, or the dog jumping on the bed—I notice that I am no longer sleeping but becoming conscious. Through repetition, I have trained myself, in this in-between state, to recognize that *I actually get to wake up this morning.* Awakening each day is not something I take for granted.

I've lived long enough to know that not everybody wakes up in the morning. I think of my friend Wayne Dyer, who went to bed on a Saturday night and never woke up. A popular author and inspirational thinker, Wayne had a calendar booked for nearly three years ahead. Many people go to bed at night and do not get up the next day, so when I do, my gratitude is profound. In the morning, I *notice* that I am waking up and immediately begin a meditation that expresses my appreciation to the Infinite for the gift of another day. Often, the feeling of gratitude comes as naturally as breathing.

Sometimes, however, I may be sad or troubled. Feeling grateful takes concentrated effort. During the COVID pandemic, far too many of us lost loved ones. My only sibling and my oldest friend passed away within six months of each other, and because of travel restrictions, I could not be with either of them in their last days.

Still, I don't let my feet hit the floor until I am fully in a state of gratitude, so that I can feel it in my body. I tell myself, "This is a one-of-a-kind, completely irreplaceable, wondrous gift of life in my hands." Whatever state I put myself in will dictate my decisions that day. It will dictate the opportunities I can see, or not see, based on the vibration I am living from. The frequency of gratitude is expansive and harmonious with abundance. You will not find greater abundance if you are tuned to a negative or complaining frequency. Abundance and complaint do not exist on the same frequency.

Not one of us is promised another day. Before I even open my eyes or put my feet on the ground, I give thanks for another day of life. Borrow my words if they help you. Or use your own. Here is what I say:

> I have been given the gift of waking up this morning.
>
> This is not just another day of my life; this is a brand-new day! And I'm going to make it an extraordinary day.
>
> Nobody gets to think my thoughts today, except me. Nobody gets to make my choices today, but me.
>
> This is a unique, one-of-a-kind, irreplaceable, completely wondrous gift of life in my hands today. I am so grateful for the opportunity to be alive and to choose who I am going to be in this day.

Practice Gratitude to Build Your Believing

As you actively practice gratitude, notice that you are marshaling your assets. When you express gratitude for your health—or at least for the parts of you that are healthy—you are acknowledging an asset. Whether I am feeling grateful for the comfortable sheets, the roof holding out the rain, my family, my education, or parents who loved me, I realize that I am enumerating my assets, that is, listing the resources needed to actively build my dreams. When you live in a state of gratitude, more opportunities present themselves to you, and you have a more expansive experience of being alive. Practicing gratitude helps you to recognize that you have more resources than you think, and that you are capable of more than you believe.

Like basketball players who mentally practice sinking free throws, you have a tremendous capacity to rewire your brain for what you desire. Several times in the past decades, experiments comparing the effects of basketball players physically practicing free throws and those of players vividly imagining themselves sinking the shot have been performed, with similar results. The players who visualized the shots improved as much or more than those who practiced physically. Physical and mental actions change the brain in similar ways. Fortify your dream by actively practicing gratitude.

Practicing gratitude is the first of three action steps, that, along with a Brave Thinking Tool, will match the frequency of your dream to align with the invisible laws of the Infinite that draw your dream from the future into the present.

Most of us were raised with what I call reactive gratitude, which is triggered by something external, like an unexpected raise at work. Similarly, you feel grateful when someone gives you a gift, pays you a compliment, or brings dinner over when you are sick. But Brave Thinkers practice a type of gratitude that comes from deep within and that keeps them thankful without needing a prompt. Should you feel gratitude only under specific circumstances, your possibilities will be limited. By contrast, what I call generative gratitude expands your vision. It puts you at a frequency that sustains a constant state of gratefulness, regardless of what is happening in your life. If I want to watch the Discovery Channel, I cannot stay tuned to CNN or the Hallmark Channel. I need to change the frequency. Gratitude encompasses far more than how we feel at a given moment. When we practice gratitude, we move into a different state of mind.

Psychologists from Southern Methodist University in Dallas, Texas, and the University of California, Davis, conducted a study about the extraordinarily positive impact of gratitude on people's overall well-being. In a series of studies entitled "The Grateful Disposition: A Conceptual and Empirical Topography," the psychologists split several hundred people into three groups. The participants agreed to write in a diary at the end of each day for the duration of the study. The first group received no instructions about what to record, and so they chose to write about whatever happened during the day, either positive or negative. The second group was instructed to write only about the day's unpleasant experiences. The third group was asked to write only about what made them feel grateful that day.

The study found that only the third group, whose members expressed their gratitude in writing daily, had higher overall levels of alertness, enthusiasm, determination, optimism, and energy. This same group also experienced less depression and stress, and were more likely to help others, exercise regularly, and make greater progress toward their personal goals. Give thanks right now, and you will be elevated to a state of consciousness that attunes you to opportunities that were there all along, ones readily missed by an ungrateful mind.

The universe bestows the good things of life in proportion to a person's readiness to receive. A person who goes to the great ocean of life feeling undeserving will take only a teaspoon. A more believing person, filled with gratitude, runs to that same ocean with a bucket, knowing the ocean delights in filling any container it is offered. Generative gratitude quiets your inner critic, builds your compassion for others, and gives you greater freedom to pursue your dream.

Give thanks right now, and you will be elevated to a state of consciousness that attunes you to opportunities that were there all along, ones readily missed by an ungrateful mind.

Gratitude quiets the voice of your inner critic

We all have an inner critic that seeks to point out our limitations or tries to tell us that we are not good enough or deserving enough to have what we want in life. But when we listen to our inner critic and mistakenly believe that it is telling us the truth, this can affect the results we produce and lower our overall quality of life. Practicing gratitude, however, is a powerful way to quiet the voice of your inner critic.

By regularly shifting your awareness to one of gratitude, you increase your sense of worthiness. This is because where focus goes, energy flows, and results show. If you choose to give your energy to constrictive, self-critical thoughts that say you are not fully deserving of what you desire, your desired results will likely always elude you. Focusing on how you or others fall short and seeing your relationships from a place of criticism can be all too easy. This way of thinking can block you from moving toward your dreams and from fully connecting with and appreciating others. At any moment, you have the choice to either criticize yourself or to appreciate the qualities you possess. If you give more energy to thoughts of gratitude, you begin to think expansively, quieting your inner critic and attracting greater joy and abundance into your life. You can forgive yourself for mistakes that you still feel foolish or shameful about and view them instead as learning opportunities to grow and change.

Gratitude builds compassion for others

When we shift our awareness to gratitude, we can better see the good not only in ourselves but in others, too, raising our natural frequency to one of compassion and connectedness. We then feel much lighter, and more relaxed, and we can move forward with increased self-love and healthier, happier relationships. This is how gratitude operates as an expansive feeling that opens the door to a happier, healthier, and wealthier life. Anyone who has ever loved another unconditionally can recall how that person appears radiant and beautiful. If we love another person fully, we may not always like their behavior, but we are always grateful to have that person in our lives.

I'll never forget a presentation I attended many years ago. Christine, an inspirational speaker, spoke of a man she knew with a bulbous nose that rivaled Jimmy Durante's famous proboscis. Every time she looked at him, all she saw was that nose. It was as if the rest of him were invisible. She didn't even notice the color of his eyes. Then one day, while looking at him critically, the thought hit her. "It's as plain as the nose on his face. I tend to look at what's wrong instead of focusing on what's right. Not just with this man's nose, either, but with my whole life." Christine began to practice gratitude for the kindness this man displayed toward her. She appreciated his intelligence, his concern for the environment, and his work ethic. Over time, the two became close friends. Then, sitting across from him one day while having coffee, she found her heart overflowing with love for him. She blurted out, "Jake, you have the most wonderful nose." His profile had not changed; the change came from within Christine. To her, his nose had become distinguished. It shrank as her heart expanded. Eventually the two married. And, yes, each of their beautiful children has a prominent proboscis.

Such a seemingly small step as not criticizing someone deepens our sense of gratitude. As we grow in gratitude we are renewed, and the energies of love literally transform our old life into the life of our dreams. Try making a list of every person you have criticized or condemned in some way during the past week. This might include a coworker, a politician, your spouse, or the nosy neighbor. Next to that person's name, write something about them for which you give thanks. The coworker whose incessant office chatter you find so annoying may also have a beautiful smile. Ask yourself if perhaps she talks so much at work because she goes home to an empty house each day. Cease your criticism. Stop expecting the worst, and you'll stop receiving it. If you are fortunate enough to have a confidante, be grateful for that. Then move on down your list. For twenty-four hours, practice exercising a grateful mind, a grateful heart. When we choose to not criticize by turning our attention to something of a higher nature, grace flows to us. As we grow in gratitude we are renewed, and the energies of love literally transform our old life into the life of our dreams.

Gratitude gives you greater freedom

When we forget to operate from a place of gratitude, we can get stuck, overlooking opportunities because we cannot see them from the frequency of doubt, worry, fear, criticism, and blame. But when we cultivate a feeling of gratitude, our minds and hearts open to everything the universe has to offer, and we operate on the frequency to fully receive and act on these ideas and opportunities. Practicing gratitude is an extraordinary way to free up an immense amount of time and energy, so that you can focus on pursuing your greatest dreams.

A man I know, Ken, adopted my practice of generative gratitude, which he says helped him to inventory his strengths and fortify his dream. He told me, "I am grateful for my family. They fill me with joy. I am grateful for my education and how it has opened many doors. I am grateful when a blessing just seems to just drop in my lap. Some of what looked like opportunity led to bad fortune, but I have had the strength to stand up one more time than I have fallen down. I am grateful for my failures, for the wider experience and humility they have given me. My practice of gratitude has lifted burdens of doubt, anxiety, and fear. I have seen that good things come to me when I expect them. I am grateful for this law of attraction because, as a result of it, I have built and continue to build my dreams. Oh, and then there is my soulmate who loves me and is strong where I am weak. I guess you could say I attracted her, too."

Notice where you are holding your dream. For most of us, it is a life we have only imagined, somewhere *out there*, which is a good place to start. But when we bring it close, we can act decisively, moment by moment, in the direction of our dream. That is how it will come alive. Brave Thinking makes realizing what you would love both enjoyable and life-giving. It does not have to feel like such a struggle. Yes, it takes hard work—but not strife. There are obstacles, and we overcome them not by striving but rather by changing our thinking, acting, and seeing how the Infinite can surprise us. Chasing down a dream and forcing it into submission is much harder than attuning your life to the vibrations that match your dream and welcoming it into your life. By maximizing the resources available to him, my son John became a powerful dream builder in a situation where there seemed to be absolutely no answer for the dream he wanted.

His Brave Thinking story began in 1991. He was twenty-four years old, casually hanging out in Cabo San Lucas, a bit lost in life, that is, until the day he found out he was going to be a father. In that moment, John decided to get serious. He told me, "I am in love with the idea of fatherhood, and I want to be a good dad." A single father to his son, Ricardo, John focused on his work in sales in the hotel industry so

BRAVE THINKING TOOL

Do what you can from where you are with what you have

he could support his little boy. And yet, there was something missing for him—a life partner, a confidante, a lover. A soulmate.

Just as I, as a teenage mother about to undergo kidney surgery, had envisioned walking him to kindergarten, John too dreamed for a woman he could love and cherish. He visualized waking up next to her every morning. Before long, he met his soulmate, Dora, bringing another of his longstanding dreams to reality. Just as I had imagined when John was a baby, I sat in the front row of his wedding, watching with pride as he married the love of his life. That's how Dora, Ricardo, and John became a family.

Then they began to dream together. Their biggest dream— and challenge—was owning their own home. In the United States, most people secure a mortgage to buy a home. In Mexico, the volatile economy precludes mortgage financing. John and Dora rented, holding out the vision for a home of their own. About a year after they were married, a developer came to Cabo, offering private financing for twelve homes he planned to build.

The couple all but ran to the developer's office but quickly turned to leave once they realized that they lacked sufficient funds for a down payment. As they were walking out of the office, the developer asked if they could simply make a deposit and secure the remainder of the down payment in nine months, when the home would be ready for occupancy.

John and Dora and talked it over. Deciding to pay the deposit was a Brave Thinking moment for the couple because they had no idea how they would find the funds for the full down payment. And yet, once they decided to go forward, the Infinite stepped in. Dora co-owned a restaurant, and it began to take off. Over the next nine months, she raised most of the money for the down payment. The family moved into their two-bedroom place that had a view of the Cabo San Lucas Bay. In John's words: "Our dream together had come true."

The couple's vision continued to expand. They dreamed of adding another child to their family and were blessed with twin girls in return: Kayla and Kiara, who spent their first two years sleeping in bassinets in their parents' bedroom. John and Dora never stopped being grateful for their home, but their dream dwelling had become cramped quarters. John began paying attention to his longing and discontent. Successful dream builders often find that they outgrow a past dream and are ready to move into something bigger, be it a new home, or a more expansive version of their present life.

John felt as if he were right back where he started: he wanted a home but had no financing. But this time, John had a great business mentor who told him, "You must be willing to do whatever it takes. Are you willing?" The financial gap between the home he was living in and anything bigger felt insurmountable to John, but he was willing.

One day, John's mentor asked him, "Do you know what the enemy of *great* is?"

John said, "I don't know. Bad?"

"No. *Good*. The enemy of *great* is *good*. Here's the deal: You have it good. You must be willing to risk the good you have if what you want is great."

For two years, John tried to finance a new house. He employed every strategy he could to make it happen and came up empty. Another discussion with his mentor revealed that, based on his current financial situation, it would take fifteen years for John's family to afford a new home.

Around this time, I went to visit my son and his family and spend time with my little granddaughters. The night before I left Cabo, I asked him, "If you could do or have anything, what would you love?"

He described his dream house and told me how the absence of mortgages in Mexico made that impossible. I reminded him about blueprinting and asked what the house would look like. He designed a literal blueprint on a napkin: the number of bedrooms and bathrooms, a play-room for the girls, a separate bedroom for Ricardo.

We calibrated his emotional state around this vision: Would he love this house? The answer was a resounding yes.

Then I asked, "What could you do from where you are with what you have?" John said he could use more support, someone to help him. That someone was me.

What John had was a napkin and a piece of land in Cabo that he'd previously invested in. I told him about Time Machine, the exercise I shared with you in chapter 4, where you imagine it is three years from now and you describe your dream in the present tense, as if it is already happening. So, every day, John went to his land with his napkin blueprint and visualized his home as if it had already manifested. In his mind, it was a form of time traveling, imagining every day what it would be like and feel like to live in his dream house.

He realized a builder would not be able to work with his blueprint on a napkin, so he spoke to an architect, who told him the plans would cost $15,000. He had money for the

John's literal blueprint on a napkin
of his dream house in Cabo San Lucas.

plans, but if he spent it on them, he would have none for the house. Still, he did what he could, from where he was, with what he had. John bought the plans, firmly committing to his dreams. Commitment is the pledge or promise you make to yourself to keep the energy flowing. You are partnering with the Infinite to be a match in frequency for the life you would love.

What else could John do from where he was with what he had? John and Dora had another very brave idea and acted on it. They put their house up for sale. This was a bold act of faith, which is where the results of Brave Thinking really come through. Then something highly unusual happened. A man wanted to buy John's house but didn't want to move in for five more years, which meant John, Dora, Ricardo, Kayla, and Kiara could stay put, renting their existing house instead of finding somewhere else to live while they built their dream home.

Then the architect told John that the money from his house sale would only lay the foundation of the new house, and perhaps the beginnings of a garage. In the spirit of Brave Thinking, John invested all his money from his former house to build the foundation and start the garage. On the day construction was scheduled to stop for lack of funds, a man drove up to ask what he was doing. It turned out this man was a financier who offered him a loan to continue building. The man worked for an investment banking company you may have heard of called Lehman Brothers. This ended up being the last home loan the company gave out before its collapse in 2008.

My son's family moved in on Thanksgiving Day, which is significant, because John and Dora have so much for which

Everything good that happened came about from John
imagining a life he would love. He and his family
moved into their dream house on Thanksgiving Day.

to be grateful, including that first home that launched their Brave Thinking journey together. Brave Thinking worked for John, and if you reread his story, you will see that everything good that happened came about from holding gratitude, imagining the life he would love, and doing what he could from where he was and with what he had.

Develop Partners in Believing

Remember the author Napoleon Hill, who spent twenty years researching the self-made millionaires of his day at the behest of Andrew Carnegie? Hill discovered that these entrepreneurs, including Henry Ford, Harvey Firestone, and Pierre Samuel DuPont, had something in common. Each man belonged to what Hill called a mastermind group. These individuals had one or two or three others who joined them in believing in a greater possibility than they presently experienced. They empowered one another. As Hill said, "No mind is complete by itself. It needs contact and association with other minds to grow and expand."

Do you have support systems in your life? John and Dora were partners in believing for one another. John also had a strong business mentor who encouraged him to step out of his comfort zone, and finally he had me, his mother, who helped him think about what he could do from where he was and with what he had.

When you gravitate toward those who affirm your potential, you cannot help but fortify your dream. Partners are those who believe in you, especially when you find it hard to believe in yourself.

If you are like me, the idea of building a group of two or more like-minded people to meet with regularly excites you. Discuss your dream with them. Let them help you document your dream and remind you to stay on course. The people with whom you associate have a dramatic influence on your life. If you spend time with people who continually tear you down, your self-worth eventually can be eroded to the point where you become convinced that what they say about you is true. Conversely, when you gravitate toward those who believe in and affirm your potential, you cannot help but fortify your dream. Partners are those who believe in you, especially when you find it hard to believe in yourself.

My best friend, Colleen, and I have been close since we met as young mothers in 1969. We have supported one another's growth and dreams through many life transitions. When the church collapsed, Colleen was there for me. There had been so many signs and signals that I didn't heed, even when Colleen tried to tell me.

Your partners in believing never judge you. They are not the people who, as you head into a dark valley, wave, and say, "I'll see you on the other side." Lots of us have friends like that, but if you are headed into a deep dark forest, your partner is a person like Colleen, who says, "Okay, I'll walk with you through this." That is a great partner in believing. They do not dictate your dreams or try to erode a dream you are trying to build. They honor your journey.

Consider people who have supported you in the past or whom you have supported. They may be close friends, or they may be casual acquaintances with whom you connect easily and who you feel have your best interests at heart, people whose ideas you have always respected, or those who have succeeded in making their own dreams come true. Chances are they didn't do it alone and will gladly pass on their learning to others. They may have a new dream that also needs some reinforcement.

A "partners in believing" group can take many forms. Sometimes each person's vision is discussed during a portion of the meeting. Sometimes an entire meeting is devoted solely to one individual. Here are a few steps to get started:

- Do progress reports. Each person states their dream and the progress made since the last meeting.

- Allow time to express discouragement so that you can purge it and move on. Others may interpret what you perceive as failure as steps toward a goal. Or if you really have regressed, let the group guide you to an alternative game plan.

- Brainstorm. Together with your partners, come up with as many suggestions as possible for you to step into your dream.

- Ask the "suppose" question: "Suppose your dream is possible. What would you do first?" Ask this question again and again, putting yourself into the mindset that with the Infinite, all things are possible.

- Follow up. Embracing greater possibility is one thing, taking steps so that the possibility comes to fruition is another. With your partners, decide which actions you will take before your next meeting. Then, the next time, review your progress with the group. If you let yourself down, you'll be letting them down, too. The prospect of disappointing people we respect is often enough to motivate most of us.

- Encourage creative thinking. Your partners may want to ask you to imagine yourself moving closer to your dream. "If you were getting closer, how would you know? What would you notice first? What in your life would be different?"

- Mark small milestones. You don't have to wait to celebrate. Acknowledging your progress, even before the dream manifests, is powerful motivation for the next step.

- Challenge limited thinking. Although you have worked strategically to create a more empowering worldview, old habits and beliefs can resurface, especially as you push past your comfort zone. Your partners in believing bring a fresh perspective that can help you get back on track.

An alternative to developing partners in believing is to work one-on-one with a coach. That's what Benny Vaughn did. A Black man born in the Deep South in the 1950s, Benny knew what it felt like to ride in the back of the bus and drink from what was called the "colored" water fountain. He was denied entry to many places in his own hometown of Columbus, Georgia.

Growing up in a city infested by longstanding racism fueled Benny's determination to succeed in life—and he did. Benny received a full track scholarship to the University of Florida as a five-star recruit. He pursued a successful career as a sports massage therapist and licensed athletic trainer. He has worked with Olympians and other elite professional athletes, helping them to perform, to win the Superbowl and NBA championships.

On the surface, Benny's life appeared a dream come true. But the demands of his work took their toll. Because of business debt and a deep commitment to his clients, he thought his only option was to work more. Benny gained forty pounds. He developed sleep apnea. He went to see his doctor, who told him to slow down. "When you die, your clients will simply find another therapist," his doctor said.

At that moment, Benny realized he needed help; he attended a DreamBuilder Live event, and I became his coach. By applying Brave Thinking Tools, Benny transformed his own life. He and his wife have strengthened their relationship. His income has increased by more than 40 percent, and for the first time in years, he and his wife have taken vacations, hiking the bush trails in New Zealand, and celebrating their thirty-third wedding anniversary in a villa in Tuscany. Benny's health has also improved. He now exercises daily and is twenty-five pounds lighter.

Benny joined me in one of our Brave Thinking Institute's spiritual retreats, which included a trip to the Henry Ford Museum in Dearborn, Michigan. There, we sat together on the Rosa Parks bus, an experience that inspired Benny's current dream. "In that moment, I realized what my mission is—to build an athletic training facility for young people who have challenges, who have also been told they can't do something because of their race, creed, or color. They will have a place where they can realize their dreams athletically and academically." Inspired by my son John's story of designing his dream home on a napkin, Benny found an architectural firm to draw up blueprints for free. As of this writing, Benny is pursuing that dream of making the athletic facility a reality.

Benny is what I call "a person of increase," someone who recognizes that service is the highest calling, and that the abundance we seek is attracted by our own generosity.

Become a Person of Increase

In 1973, I was attending seminary, Haven was working as a truck driver, and we had a five-year-old and a six-year-old. We were a struggling young family. My life had become more complicated since that fateful healing when I was eighteen, but I wanted to keep growing in my understanding of transformation. I attended a conference in Los Angeles where Raymond Charles Barker was speaking. I had heard that this leader in the New Thought church knew how to translate Infinite potential into real results and always attracted huge crowds. This day was no exception. He stepped onstage, an elderly man with white hair and a snappy double-breasted suit. Then he reached into his pocket, pulled out his wallet, and spread handfuls of hundred-dollar bills on a table for us to see.

"This is money," he said. "I love money."

Immediately, I felt repulsed, judging the man for being greedy. I couldn't believe I had driven all that way and waited in line for *this*. Then he said, "I imagine many of you were disgusted by what I just did. You may have judged me." It was as though he had reached right inside my mind and heard exactly what I was thinking and feeling. "But tell me," he said, "How would money flow to a person who doesn't love it?"

I still wasn't buying it. Then he continued: "If I had walked out here, and instead of reaching into my wallet to show you money, I picked up my five-year-old grandson and said, 'I love my grandson,' you all would have applauded. Why? Because you have been programmed to believe it's okay to love a grandchild but not okay to love the symbol of your own freedom."

He was right. I longed to be what I now call "a person of increase," someone who draws to them the skills, supportive community, ideas, and financial means to bring their dreams to life. With an abundance mindset, all of these things will flow to you. Appreciating your own abundance attracts greater abundance, not just materially, but in the form of ideas, people, and experiences to fortify your dream. If you are a person of increase, you feel gratitude both for what you already have as well as what you desire to manifest. My son John became a person of increase by putting himself in a position that called for unknown sources to achieve his dream.

Try this experiment: Take a deep breath and hold it. Do not breathe. Hold it a little longer. Pull in a little more. Hold on to that breath. This is your life. This is all the good that you have now. Hang on to it. Don't release one drop. Keep holding it.

You know what happens if you never let go? You will either exhale or become unconscious. That is what happens to many of us. We have become unconscious because we have not learned how to let go. We cling to what we have, thinking that we can run our lives ourselves. When we move into the illusion of self-will, we become oblivious to something bigger—the Infinite—and to spiritual law in our lives. So many of us want only to inhale, to take. We forget that the life-giving act of breathing itself requires us to exhale, to give in equal measure. Circulation is required, breathing in and breathing out. We become a person of increase through circulation, recognizing that we live in a generous universe and practicing conscious generosity every day. Giving activates receiving.

Bless the good you have and share a portion of it. Fill the world around you with a portion of your worth and you yourself become replenished. The Infinite fills your life according to the dimensions of your belief. Abundance evolves through giving. A person of increase is one who shares his or her own wealth. As you replenish the world around you with a portion of your worth, remember it is your world that you are moving forward. If you are going to accelerate in a car, first you fill it with fuel; if you want heat from a wood stove, first you put in the wood. It does no good to stand outside the stove screaming, "Give me some heat and I'll give you some wood!" And yet we often treat the universe that way. To accelerate your life, give. Tell yourself, "Every moment I'm all in. I practice being a person of increase, bringing increased aliveness and kindness to the world."

The universe can only do for us what it does through us. We make room for additional good in our lives. We practice being a person of increase through every interaction, using words that are constructive and life-giving with our family, coworkers, employees, and others who cross our path each day.

For example, suppose someone cuts you off in traffic. Many of us immediately feel resentful. Maybe we speed up and try to cut that driver off and put him in his place. Rather than get even, we could tell ourselves, "This guy must be really in a hurry. I'm going to give him a bit more room." Or consider how you communicate with the clerk at the grocery store. While the checkout clerk is scanning your purchases, are you talking on your cell phone or engaging with the person whose work is helping you to put dinner on the table tonight? You can have a moment of increase by inquiring about their day or expressing appreciation for their work or how they go about it. "Every time I'm here, I notice you always have a big smile on your face." Or "Thank you for bagging my groceries. They're going to be easy for me to carry this way." A person of increase consciously tries to touch the lives of others. Even a seemingly small gesture or acknowledgment can make a difference.

We all get twenty-four hours a day. Each person receives the same amount of that abundance—525,600 minutes in a year. You and I get to choose how we are going to use those units of life. Some of us will unconsciously choose to invest 30,000 units in an old resentment, building up a big wall of a grudge without realizing that that investment pays negative dividends. Others who invest in gratitude, appreciation, and giving receive dividends in the form of greater abundance.

I'd like to close this chapter by telling you about a woman from my former congregation, Nancy, a person of increase who taught me a lesson in abundance I will never forget. I helped Nancy plan her sixtieth birthday party. She sent invitations to all her friends. "This is my last birthday," she wrote, "so please bring me something very, very special." Her friends knew this to be the truth. Nancy was dying of cancer.

The day of her party, Nancy sat with friends gathered around her and slowly, gratefully opened every present. There was a beautiful scarf, and she tried it on, relishing the luxury of the silk. She opened a candle and inhaled the delicate floral scent. Then she laid all her presents out on the table and looked around at her friends. "Right now, I'm not in a gathering period in my life; I'm in a relinquishing period, and I'm learning how beautiful this can be. What I want is for each of you to select a gift that you did not bring and take that gift home with you. All the years you live, remember my love for you whenever you see this gift."

Nancy died six weeks later. Her days were fewer than she, her friends, and her family would have wanted, yet her life was abundantly full. Your life can be, too.

FORTIFYING YOUR DREAM

Brave Thinking Tool: Do what you can from where you are with what you have
Marshal your assets, engaging your existing resources to take steps in building your dream, recognizing that the Infinite is intelligent and responsive to your thoughts, feelings, and actions.

Teaching points

*   Practice gratitude to build your believing. As you live in a state of gratitude, more opportunities present themselves, and over time self-criticism becomes quieter.

*   Develop at least one partner in believing, someone like you, who has a vivid dream. Together you can provide one another with support, accountability, and motivation for your dream-building journey.

*   Become a person of increase. Approach every interaction seeking to benefit others and you will attract greater good into your own life.

OPENING TO THE UNEXPECTED DREAM

"There is no problem outside of you that is superior to the power within you."

BOB PROCTOR

Always, finally,

"This or something better, still."

Open at the top.

EVERY TIME MY cell phone rang, I felt a little spark of hope that the call would be an invitation for me to speak at an event. A year had passed since the collapse of the church I had built, and with it, the end of my ministry. Unemployed, I counted on income from speaking engagements to make payments on the enormous debt I was determined to bring to zero. But in those days, I didn't receive many invitations.

So when the board president of the Big Sky Retreat, Joe Dickey, invited me to speak at the organization's 2005 event, I was thrilled. Many years earlier, I had met Joe and his late wife, Robin, at various events. Our circles overlapped and we had many colleagues in common. The annual weeklong retreat in Big Sky, Montana, brings together spiritual thinkers and seekers who share a common passion for personal transformation. My former long-time assistant, Ginger, joined me.

The retreat required my full energy and focus, so I had been looking forward to the afternoon off that the speakers had been promised. I couldn't wait to curl up with a good book. Then Joe told me that the board members traditionally spent their afternoon off at Firehole River in Yellowstone, where they would take part in a Native American ritual that involved lying on a bed of rocks in shallow water as the gentle current washed over you.

"The current releases everything you want to let go," he said. "It is a very powerful experience. Would you like to join us?"

"Cold is my least favorite thing," I replied. "Besides, I didn't bring a swimsuit, so I'm going to pass. But thank you for inviting me."

The next day, he approached me with a big smile on his face. "Guess what?" he said. "The wife of one of our board members brought a second swimsuit, and you can borrow it!"

Had this woman not packed an extra suit, my life would look very different than it does today.

The river trip was restorative. I had felt so beaten up inside, grieving the loss of my dream and the life I had loved. The cold water flowing over my body reminded me that even that which is temporary contains great power. The church no longer existed physically, but the energy and love that built my dream had not gone anywhere. I began to let go, if only a little.

When the retreat ended, Ginger and I drove to the airport. In the car, she asked, "Mary, could you get interested in Joe Dickey?"

"Absolutely not!" I ticked off my priorities: spending time with my children and grandchildren; rebuilding my career; paying off a seemingly impossible debt. I didn't say it, but Ginger knew: more than anything, I needed to protect my wounded heart. Married at sixteen, I had spent twenty-seven years with a wonderful man, but we never developed the kind of deep connection I longed for in a soulmate. My second marriage was ultimately devastating, destroying the church I had spent more than two decades building.

Ginger sighed, "I'm just going to say that when I saw the two of you presenting onstage together at the retreat, it was magic."

"Good for you," I replied. And that was that.

Then Joe emailed to thank me for participating in the retreat. For three weeks, I didn't respond, but we eventually struck up an email friendship. At one point, he said, "We could get a lot more said if we actually spoke to one another." Forget the phone call, I told him. I knew where he was headed, and I was not going down that path again.

Joe called anyway. We soon found ourselves talking for hours on end. Then one day, he emailed to say that he had seen on my website that I'd be giving a presentation in Los Angeles, not far from where he lived.

"When you're in Los Angeles, I'd like to take you to dinner," he wrote.

I wrote back, "No, that's too much like a date."

He replied, "Mary, it's just dinner…"

"Someday I'll write a book titled *It's Never Just Dinner*." But I said yes.

Joe was raising two adorable children, whom I met that weekend when we had our first dinner together. He was a wonderful man, an accomplished author and performer. After his wife passed away in 1999, he cut back his singing work to be at home with his eight-year-old daughter and four-year-old son. He juggled a musical career with chauffeuring, shopping, cooking, washing, and ironing. He even won a "Single Parent of the Year Award." Still, I feared risking love and repeating my past mistakes. A few months later,

I was speaking in Los Angeles again. Joe invited me to come by his house for coffee, and then he'd take me lunch. He provided directions to his home in the Simi Valley, northwest of Los Angeles. I drove through the magnificent Santa Susana Pass for the first time, a nine-mile-long stretch of valley with mountains on either side.

Coming down the hill, I heard a voice say, "I could live here." That voice was so distinct I looked around, wondering, "Who said that? Where did that come from?" This was, in fact, my still, small voice—that gift from the Infinite that speaks calmly and uncritically, transforming random intuition into inspired insight. My inner self already knew what my outer self had resisted, that this relationship was meant to be.

The unexpected dream can take many forms. This was a dream I had pushed away, even as the universe nudged me toward my highest good. The unexpected dream can also cause fear and doubt. You may have created a specific vision of a life you would love, only for events to take a bewildering turn. Or the dream may manifest differently than you imagined, rendering it unrecognizable at first.

Dream-building isn't a paint-by-numbers process. Take heart that when "it"—your dream—is coming together, things can get messy, even confounding. Just as physicists' view of the unpredictability of nature has evolved in recent decades to recognize that apparent randomness contains order, the dream that appears chaotic may be coming together in a cohesive manner. Deterministic chaos theory has shown that the structure emerging from the chaos is highly dependent on the initial conditions of the system. In our case this translates as relating to how well we prepare the dream for action. If you set the initial conditions with a tested, fortified dream, shifted your paradigms, and have

BRAVE THINKING TOOL

This is what *it* looks like when *it* is all coming together

become a person of increase, your dream will manifest, perhaps in an unexpected way. Or the universe may be guiding you to a greater dream.

As I shared earlier, I cared deeply for my first husband, but we were never soulmates. My dream had always been for a spiritual partnership, where two souls blended into one, the kind of profoundly loving relationship my parents enjoyed. Then my second marriage shut down my heart, so I kept love at a distance, which limited all aspects of my life, including the willingness to trust and the opportunity to grow. Opening a wounded heart risks more pain but is required for a more expansive, abundant life. By turning my attention from what frightened me to what I would love, I awakened one morning to the startling revelation that my dream had come true after all.

Two years after Joe corralled that bathing suit from a board member's wife, we were married. Today, we have a beautiful, blended family, created by continuing to sew love, connection, and unconditional acceptance. I have not only my own adult children but amazing bonus kids with Joe, and the privilege of helping to raise them and being blessed by their presence. As of this writing, Joe and I have a combined seven adult children and twelve grandchildren.

The dream can also manifest in an unexpected form. I know a man who, as a young boy, dreamed of being an industrialist, not that he really knew what an industrialist did. But he had a clear vision of himself looking out the window from an office in a big building he had built, surveying a factory of happy workers. He saw smokestacks, a railyard, and all that he had created. He said he was trying to answer for his young mind a question about how he would fit into the world in a way that mattered. A captain of industry was not a vocation he pursued, but the vision of himself looking out that window never faded.

One day, decades later, he found himself standing in his home office, looking out the third-story window of his house, thinking of the trees he had cleared for the site of the house, remembering how he sawed the timbers and beams to build the home with his own hands. He looked out at the one-acre pond behind the dam that he and his first wife had built with a tractor and a bulldozer; the pond where his children learned to swim, spending summers gleefully tumbling into the water from the rope swing; the pond where a herd of shy elk often came to cool off when they thought no one was watching. He saw the fifty-foot fir trees shading the pond, and remembered them as the small trees his children had once gathered around each Christmas in the living room as they opened their presents.

He looked out at the small amphitheater he had built in hopes his daughter would marry there, and the little stage where her brothers had officiated the ceremony. He recalled dancing the hora at his stepson's reception and the annual church picnics where families, at the behest of their children, pitched tents the night before to get a head start on the festivities. He recalled backyard campouts with his children and their high school friends. He saw himself, his aging dog Shadow in his arms, trekking through the woods she had loved to roam. He thought of the family gatherings that brought together his children and grandchildren, gatherings that fostered a warm friendship between his wife, and his former wife and her partner. And he imagined the many gatherings to come.

Finally, it dawned on him. What he had built was an inclusive place of welcome and refuge that brought people together. He had built community. The Infinite had directed him to his highest good.

Tell Yourself, "This or Something Better..."

The unexpected dream can be one you initially resist or one that manifests in a manner you never anticipated. But what happens when your dream takes an abrupt detour? Are you headed for failure? Suppose you attempt to follow all the steps in this book. You invest time, energy, your very soul. Through faith and hard work, you overcome obstacles and pull yourself out of every mental ditch along the roadway. Yet the dream continues to elude you. Of any dream-building phase, the most difficult to accept and work through is failure. Still, failure can be an integral part of achieving a great dream. All people who spend their lives building a dream have known great disappointment along the way. In any dream, there may come a point at which you are tempted to give up. The reality to which you devoted your heart and energy has yet to materialize. This is a critical crossroads. If you've reached the point of diminishing returns, such as the time Haven and I kept farming only to harvest more debt, you may be better off pursuing another dream.

Before you declare defeat, take inventory. As Henry Ford once said, "When everything seems to be going against you, remember that the airplane takes off against the wind, not with it." Don't stop just before the miracle. When your dream is coming together, it can feel chaotic, even scary. As you get closer, the stakes get higher, and the risk of failure looms larger. You've come all this way and the prospect of imminent collapse, especially if your dream takes a bewildering turn, raises doubts, and increases your fear.

Now is the time to reexamine and reaffirm the beliefs and desires that brought you this far. Remember that failure is not the enemy; it is a stepping stone to success. You can rise from failure. Becoming paralyzed by fear means you cannot move. If you fear failure more than you love your dream, you avoid extending yourself at the precise moment the dream requires your bravest thinking. When you proceed confidently, accepting the possibility of failure in any dream can be a strength. My son John took a risk with his dream home, knowing his family might wind up with nothing more than a foundation and a half-finished garage. Had he given into that fear, he may not have become a Brave Thinker of the magnitude he is today. His story, and the napkin on which John drew that dream home—a napkin that he still possesses—would not have inspired thousands of others to pursue their dreams, including Benny Vaughn, who is determined to build an athletic facility to help underprivileged young people to recognize their own inherent worth.

Ask the Infinite, "If this dream is for my highest good, increase my passion for it and show me a way. If this dream is not meant to be, redirect me. This or something better."

In the lives of all dream builders, there are moments when they don't know whether to abandon or endure. When you reach that confusing point, take inventory. Ask for guidance to determine if you are giving up on your dream too early and if you are seeing it from the highest perspective. Ask the Infinite, "If this dream is for my highest good, increase my passion for it and show me a way. If this dream is not meant to be, redirect me. This or something better."

The phrase "this or something better" is my way of acknowledging cocreation with the Infinite. As cocreators, we shape the thinking that molds our dream to the highest good we can perceive at any given moment. At the same time, we recognize that our own perception of that highest good is limited. If I say, "It's what I want or nothing at all," I cannot access direction from a source of unlimited knowledge.

If you proceed confidently in the direction of your dream and it does not come to pass, know that the Infinite has something better in store for you and allow yourself to be redirected. When you are tempted to give up, you may be redirected, or you may be granted the stamina to persevere. "This or something better" are the final words to each of my prayers. If I am pursuing a dream that conflicts with my greater good, then the dream is not one I truly desire. Perhaps your perceived "failure" is simply feedback to guide you in altering your approach or refueling your engine.

We do not create every circumstance we experience, but we do create our experience of every circumstance we encounter. We all have what I call a "response-ability." The ability to respond however we choose, regardless of our loss, is the Infinite's gift to us. Sometimes perspective can mean the difference between success and failure. Perspective determines the opportunities we see and the choices we make, and the way we experience any outcome. I remember reading a story about the 1976 Special Olympics in Seattle. Nine contestants had lined up at the starting line for the one-hundred-yard dash. The starting gun fired, and the children took off running. One child, however, stumbled and fell. Two of the racers heard him crying. They stopped in their tracks, turned around, and saw the little boy in tears, sitting on the track. In an instant they ran back to the starting line and helped the little boy to his feet. The three of them linked arms and walked their way to the one-hundred-yard mark. The fastest runner took home a trophy that day. But as the three who crossed the finish line last smiled victoriously, the crowd cheered for them as enthusiastically as it had for the child who crossed the finish line first.

Retest Your Dream

When it comes to manifesting an unexpected dream, there's nobody quite like Diana Nyad, who at age sixty-four made history by swimming from Cuba to Florida without a shark cage. Her epic achievement took fifty-three grueling hours as she endured 111 miles of jellyfish, turbulence, and the memory of four prior attempts. In the 1970s, Diana was the world's top long-distance swimmer. At twenty-eight years old, and in peak form, she attempted this Mount Everest of all swims, only to fail. She did not swim another stroke for the next thirty years. Diana's spectacular life journey is a testament to the power of the human spirit, and I was thrilled to have her speak at one of our DreamBuilder Live events.

Diana grew up near the ocean in Fort Lauderdale, Florida. When she was five years old, her father told her the origin of the family name, Naiad, in Greek mythology referred to the nymphs that swam in the lakes, rivers, and oceans to protect the gods. He predicted that Diana would be a champion swimmer one day. "It is your destiny!" he told her. When she was a nine-year-old, Diana became a child champion pool swimmer. In 1953, the Cuban revolution broke out. Overnight, thousands of Cubans flooded to her hometown. Diana grew up with a deep appreciation for Cuban culture, flying the Cuban flag, eating Cuban food, and dancing salsa in the living room. One day on the beach, she asked her mother, "Where's Cuba?"

"It's just across the horizon." Her mother pointed, adding, "You little swimmer, you could almost swim there."

At that moment, something fluttered in Diana's imagination and settled there. In 1978, she attempted the swim. "My attitude was sharks, jellyfish, summer storms, get out of my way." But after nearly forty-two hours of eight-foot seas and a night of vomiting, she gave up. At age thirty, she retired from swimming and became a successful sports broadcaster, a career she greatly appreciated, but over time, made her feel like a spectator. "I wasn't chasing my own dreams," she told us. "I was telling the story of other people chasing their dreams."

When Diana was sixty, her mother passed away. Diana decided to "live large" from that moment on. After thirty years on dry land, Diana decided, "I'm going to chase that Cuba dream."

As Diana shared her story with us, I noticed how, from the time she was five years old, she paid attention to signs and signals, beginning with her father's prophecy that she was destined to become a champion swimmer. The night before her fifth and final attempt to swim from Miami to Cuba was no different. Here is how Diana tells it, in her own words.

> I can't sleep. I walk the streets of Key West and go into an all-night drug store. There's only one shopper inside. He's Cuban, knows my story, and he told me his story. When he was seven, his family fled Cuba on a windy night on a half-inflated, dilapidated raft. He was scared to death, thinking the raft won't make it past the break-water, much less one hundred miles of open ocean. His family called this water the Cuban graveyard. Many of their friends and family had not made it across to free-dom in the middle of the night.

> His grandmother came down to the shore and pulled him off to the side. "*Mi querido*," she said, "I'm not going. This is my country. I'm too old, but listen to me, an American once gave me this two-dollar bill. They say it means good luck over there. I'm going to zip it in your jacket. It's going to help you survive the crossing and make a new life in America and, *mi querido*, it's possible that you and I will never see each other again. Here's the caveat with this two-dollar bill. One day, you're going to meet somebody who really needs some good luck and you're going to give them this two-dollar bill the way I'm giving it to you tonight."

> On the night before my fifth attempt, the Cuban in the drugstore gave me his two-dollar bill. I took it with me all the way across the ocean.

Retest your dream. In reviewing the five questions you asked yourself before committing to the dream, you may find support in unexpected places and discover that you are not as far afield as you imagined. You can ask yourself another series of questions.

Question #1: Does the dream still enliven me?

For the moment, carefully set aside feelings of doubt or fear that may be masking your enthusiasm. Perhaps your passion for the dream has dwindled; however, fear, distraction, and even success in other aspects of your life may have pushed your passion aside. Diana Nyad buried her passion for swimming so deeply that she did not swim a stroke for three decades.

Question #2: Will continuing to pursue this dream align with my core values?

One of Diana's core values is resilience. It empowered her to undertake a fifth attempt at a seemingly impossible swim. "I have the courage to fail," she said. "When you get knocked down, you get back up. Whatever your dream is, one day, you will arrive at that other shore, whatever that shore may be."

Question #3: Do I need to grow more into my true self?

You've made it this far. Perhaps you need only to stretch a little further. After more than thirty years out of water, Diana was unsuccessful in three attempts to swim from Cuba to Florida. In fact, the media pretty much gave up on her. CNN had been on the story for four years and called to say they were terribly sorry but did not have the resources to follow her on this journey once again. They didn't think that Diana or anyone else could succeed. The *New York Times*, the *Washington Post*, and others responded similarly. Diana called the reporters to offer thanks for the respect they had shown her team over the years. But she also recognized that, at age sixty-four, she was still growing and up for the challenge. "The success of this quest revolves around one thing," she told them, "the power of the human spirit. Because of the power of the human spirit, we will make it up to that other shore."

Question #4: Do I still need help from a Higher Power to make this dream come true?

As doubts arise, we cling more tightly to our attempts to control every detail. Leave room for the Infinite to work through you. In the first year of my marriage to Joe, back in 2007, we had a weekend getaway in a cabin. One morning we were sitting on a little deck, drinking coffee in our bathrobes and listening to a babbling brook. Never had I been so happy in a relationship. My gratitude was overflowing. Then as I went inside to take a shower, I noticed one of Joe's socks lying in the middle of the living room floor. In an instant, I went from grateful to fearful. "Maybe this is a new trend. I thought he was so organized. What if he isn't who I thought he was all along?" As you step out beyond your comfort zone, all kinds of inner voices assail you. My dream had come true, but I didn't trust a kind of happiness I had never known. My paradigms were firing all kinds of accusations at me, telling me what I should worry about or find wrong with the situation. Feeling that much joy was apparently uncomfortable for those old stories. We all maintain a worry quotient and a happiness quotient. Your paradigms try to pull you back to the familiar, to the old you—not just once but over and over. It seemed I had found myself feeling "too happy" and "not worried enough" and needed to correct that. I collected myself, took a deep breath, and asked the Infinite for guidance, receiving a simple, but powerful message. "Yes, it is okay to be this happy."

Question #5: Will continuing to pursue this dream ultimately bless others?

Diana's world-record crossing and her mantra, "Find a way," has inspired people of all ages to not give up on their dreams, but her journey is especially poignant for older adults. Shortly before she launched her triumphant swim, she said, "When I walk up on that shore in Florida, I want millions of those AARP sisters and brothers to look at me and say, 'I'm going to go write that novel I thought it was too late to do. I'm going to go work in Africa on that farm where those people need help. I'm going to adopt a child. It's not too late. I can still live my dreams."

Imagine the Good You Can Do

An authentic dream blesses others, in ways we can foresee when we test or retest our dream, and in ways we had never imagined. A dear friend of mine, Cynthia Kersey, was invited to a women's conference in Kenya where she was deeply moved when she heard about the plight of young girls in developing countries, girls who would go through life with no formal education. Instead, they spent their days walking miles to fetch water from the nearest source, which was often unsanitary and made them ill. Cynthia believes that education is a fundamental right and she wanted to start a foundation that would give these children a greater opportunity in life. About to celebrate her fiftieth birthday, she decided to invite everyone she knew, asking them to make a donation that would jumpstart her foundation.

I asked the level of income she would require for the first year, and she estimated $120,000. I recommended that we bring together ten people to give $1,000 a month to launch her dream.

"Would you be one of those people?" she asked. Coincidentally, I had my own dream, to become a philanthropist, but not just yet. At this moment, I could not afford that kind of dream. I hesitated a moment and then committed. The Infinite doesn't consult our timetable, but I knew the power of an unexpected dream and put $1,000 on my credit card.

What Cynthia decided to name Unstoppable Foundation is a humanitarian nonprofit that brings sustainable education to children and impoverished communities. The organization takes a holistic approach to providing education as well as removing barriers that impoverish children. Unstoppable Foundation provides health care, clean water, nutritious food, and leadership development. I am proud to say that clients and staff of my Brave Thinking Institute have donated well over $2 million to this amazing organization. Every day when my feet hit the ground, I know that children I will never meet will have a far better life because I am part of something so much bigger than just me.

So many Brave Thinkers have expanded good in the world through the manifestation of their dreams and in ways they never expected. Carol Currier, a physician, was burned out by her work. Devoting endless hours to caring for her patients, she neglected to take care of herself. Now, she was committed to finding the time to do so. She decided to sell her medical practice for $20,000. When I asked her what she would really love, she agreed that $500,000 was a better price. Not long after, Carol was offered $1.2 million for her practice. She then had the time and money freedom to exercise regularly, and her health improved dramatically. In her late sixties, she decided to pursue a passion that once seemed beyond her reach. Carol worked with chimpanzees in the Congo and orangutans in Borneo. She even spent time with Jane Goodall. Carol traveled to Nicaragua as part of a team working with an orphanage, and to Ecuador as part of a medical group, practicing medicine in parts of the country where few doctors existed.

Brave Thinking expands every aspect of our lives, showing us the power within us to better our communities. I am so thrilled by the many ways Brave Thinkers have made a difference in a corner of the world that matters to them. They have created businesses with a welcoming, inclusive environment such that employees look forward to going to work each day. They volunteer on the boards of civic, cultural, and charitable organizations. They support youth activities, further the missions of charities that inspire them, and stand for social justice. Brave Thinkers give their time to serve meals in soup kitchens and teach struggling students to read. And, like Jubril Wilson, now a successful real estate broker who helps prospective agents to study for their exams, our Brave Thinkers use their expertise to support others in building their dreams.

Imagine the good you can do. The possibilities are endless.

OPENING TO THE UNEXPECTED DREAM

Brave Thinking Tool: This is what *it* looks like when *it* is all coming together

Dream-building can get messy at times, even confounding. But as in physics, if you have set the initial conditions with a clear and tested dream, and if you stay in harmony with your dream, then order will come about, perhaps in an unexpected way. Your prevalent pattern of thinking will manifest in your life.

Teaching points

- Tell yourself, "This or something better." Your dream may show up differently than expected, or you may be guided to a still greater dream.

- Retest your dream with the five questions you first asked yourself in chapter 4. You may find support in unexpected places and discover that you are not as far afield as you imagined. Tune in to your burning desire for a life you would love and use that fire as fuel to keep going.

- Imagine the good you can do with your heightened awareness and increased sense of abundance.

11

ACTIVATING BRAVE THINKING

---

*"Never interrupt someone doing
what you said couldn't be done."*

AMELIA EARHART

_____

I am the one who...

The step to take today is...

This is my new life.

_____

T O CLIMB Mount Everest takes about forty days to reach the peak. Once you leave base camp, there are three more camps along the way. Thus far in our journey of dream-building, we have reached the last camp before the ascent to the summit. Imagine the view. Below you the glaciers and peaks of the Himalayas stretch to the horizon. Above you looms the summit. Your pulse quickens with anticipation. This chapter will equip you with a Brave Thinking action plan that will give you additional momentum to reach the pinnacle that is your dream. Climbers leaving the base camp at Everest know that after arriving at each of the next three camps, they will return to the previous camp several times for training, acclimatization, and supplies. Like them, you will return to different Brave Thinking Tools throughout your journey.

Let's take a moment to recognize your progress. At base camp, you were introduced to Brave Thinking as a system of transformation and learned it would take a shift of beliefs and a set of daily practices to create the change you want in your life. At camp one, "Blueprinting," you turned your attention away from self-defeating thoughts, freeing yourself to recognize the deep desires of your heart. Then you were ready to ask yourself that critical question, "What would I love?" You created a vision statement so vivid that you could imagine yourself already living your dream. What successful climber has not imagined themselves standing on the mountain peak with a cool breeze ruffling their hair? At camp two, "Bridging," you learned that fear and doubt cause many people to abandon their dream. To continue your journey, you used science- and technology-based principles to systematically expand your thinking to bridge the gap between what you truly desire and what you believe possible. Equipped with a blueprint for a life you would love and a welcoming environment to grow your dream, you arrived at camp three, "Building," where you take positive action, ascending to a realm where the impossible becomes possible.

A critical tool for your Building phase is the Brave Thinking Activation Process, an action plan that equips you with additional energy and direction for this phase of your dream-building expedition. This process is a proven, five-step framework to create mental clarity, build momentum, and proceed in an organized and thoughtful manner. Accessing the spiritual in a practical way, you develop a plan that allows you to consciously connect to Infinite Intelligence and build that muscle of reliance on unseen forces. This tool helps you generate ideas from the side of your nature that is Infinite, because you are being asked to put judgment aside and just write. Rather than relying on logic, you open to your higher mental faculties. The process distills what actions to take now, and in the future, holding yourself accountable. And just like the climber ascending

BRAVE THINKING TOOL

Brave Thinking Activation Process

Mount Everest who wisely returns to previous camps to acclimatize and stock up on supplies, you can revisit this action plan for nourishing ideas as often you need.

To fully engage the activation process, you'll want to put yourself in a state of calm confidence, maintaining that state throughout the exercise. As you know, focusing on your doubts puts you in a contracted state, which can only produce Common-Hour Thinking. We have decades of programming that tells us conditions rule our lives. We adhere to those conditions and struggle with the circumstances. Brave Thinking is all about taking your attention off what we call "practical" and holding a vision, even when circumstances don't yet match.

But you can't just sit there and visualize. The Brave Thinking Activation Process allows you to download steps that can, over time, realign your circumstances and attract resources you could never imagine. In the Old Testament, the psalmist David wrote, "Thy word is a lamp unto my feet." David, as a young shepherd, traveled through the mountains at night with the Israelites to avoid the daytime heat. Their path was hilly and rocky, and they had no map to follow. They strapped small lamps to their ankles so they could see the next step. You, too, are downloading a path from the Infinite one step at a time, trusting the process.

Connect to your vision and the vibration of it coming to fruition. Imagine yourself living inside your dream, as if the life you love has already manifested. Can you feel joy, peace, and gratitude in this moment? Your energy has a generative and creative impact on how you experience reality. This process breathes life into the state you need to inhabit and exude to become that person who lives in your vision. When you reach that state, you are ready to begin asking intelligent questions of the Infinite. As you know, it helps to be specific with your search terms. For example, googling "soup recipes" will overwhelm you with millions of results you don't need or want. So when I want to make a version of my favorite soup, I search for "clam chowder with littleneck clams recipe."

Source

You begin the activation process with questions. To "source" ideas from the Infinite, you pose your questions, remaining open to all the ideas you receive in response. Refrain from "why" or "how" questions. Instead, use "what" or "who" questions. Ask yourself:

1   What can I do from where I am with what I have to move me in the direction of my dream this month?

2   What are the steps I can take this week?

3   What can I do in five minutes? (I'm a believer in the five-minute power move. It's amazing how much energy you can move at times as you generate a list of things you can do in five minutes and start acting on them. It's all about building momentum.)

4   Who do I need to be to match the vibration of my dream?

Be nonjudgmental and do not edit as you hear the ideas that come in response. The first currency of the universe comes in the form of ideas. They are valuable. Jot down every idea that comes to mind. Imagine pumping water from a well. The first few pumps may be murky or brack-ish. They are old ideas, but once you've emptied yourself of what you already know, the water eventually clears, opening you to a full and pure flow of inspiration.

Years ago, I needed $50,000 to hire a recording studio to create a program for my coaching business. Applying the Brave Thinking Activation Process, I asked, "What can I do to earn an additional $10,000 this month?" One idea that came to mind: "I could work at Burger King three nights a week." Rather than telling myself, "The math doesn't add up," I wrote down "Burger King," knowing that criticizing or editing your ideas as they come out cuts off the flow. Soon I received another idea, "Host a weekend training for twenty people at $500 each." In less than a month I secured the first $10,000 and went on to hire the studio and record the program in 2009. That program continues to this day to help people, and to grow my business, as well. Most of us are trained to think that only working harder will give us greater success when all we really need is to work in harmony with how the Infinite operates in producing results.

Sort

This isn't the usual kind of sorting where you look to your Common-Hour Thinking to decide if an idea is good or bad. So how do you choose which ideas to select? Pay attention to how you resonate with each as you review them. You may have become accustomed to making such practical choices that you haven't always known how much an enlivening idea could propel you forward. If you feel restricted or indifferent about an idea, it's not for you. Focus instead on those that feel expansive. Does your pulse quicken when you imagine yourself implementing this idea? A good idea allows you to feel expansive. You've been using this system of sorting your whole life without even realizing it. Now, you want to hone that ability. Focus on the ideas that have "electricity" in them. No idea is too preposterous or impractical to consider.

I remember one woman whose dream was to attend a special event for her grandchildren, but she needed $5,000 for the trip. As she composed her list of ideas, she heard the words "move the couch." At first, she was tempted to ignore this one. How could moving a piece of furniture generate $5,000? Had her mind wandered to an overdue spring cleaning? But she wanted to be a good steward of the ideas that came to her, without judging or belittling them. A few weeks later, as she was reviewing her list, she saw "move the couch" again. Despite the illogical nature of the idea, it still had energy, so out came the sofa. And there, pushed up against the wall, was an original *Star Wars* T-shirt her son had given her years ago during a holiday gathering. But when the family was leaving the party, no one could find the shirt. Earlier in the day, they had burned extra boxes in the fireplace, and they assumed that the valuable T-shirt had gone up in smoke.

At this point, the T-shirt was worth $7,500. Preposterous ideas invented the light bulb, put a man on the moon, and set a four-minute mile. Imagining the impossible is what Brave Thinkers do.

Pay attention to each idea and ask yourself, "Could this move me at all in the direction of my dream, even a little bit?" If the answer is yes, put a star next to that idea. You are sorting ideas by how expansive or contractive they feel. Focus on what feels expansive.

Focus on the ideas that have "electricity" in them. No idea is too preposterous or impractical to consider.

Select

Create a list of the ideas that you starred based on their potential to move you in the direction of your dream. You are now going to select the order in which to act on them.

Read your starred ideas and rank them in numerical order, working from the premise that you are seeking to move in the direction of your dream. The criteria are up to you. Perhaps you instinctively prioritize the idea you first starred. Or you might choose the suggestion that you find easiest to act on. Perhaps you rate ideas by how expansive they make you feel. What's most important is that the order makes sense to you and has some "electricity" to it.

Schedule

Ask yourself, "What could I do before the end of the month?" Decide what you're going to do, estimate how much time the action will require, and determine what resources you might need to accomplish it. Then call up your calendar and block out the time. Most people prioritize making doctor's appointments over planning out their life: this is an appointment you make with your dream. Set it and keep it. Schedule the next three actions you will do to move in the direction of your dream.

Serve

Your fifth and final step is to serve. All great dream builders do this. They learn to treat little actions with great reverence. You are a part of something significant and meaningful, serving the dream set before you and having the privilege of helping others to build their own. Notice how you treat the first scheduled activity on your list. If you take your appointment casually, you will generate casual results. Chapter 6 described the power of focus and commitment. When you focus your attention, you direct energy. Committing is a pledge to yourself to sustain that flow of energy, putting your integrity on the line. As you consider each action, ask yourself, "Am I treating this action as a critical element of my dream becoming my life?" If you know that to be true, honor your commitment by following through. Treat this task with reverence, as if you were hosting your hero for dinner. Don't worry about perfection. Just know that if you step up your energy, you can move molecules. Bring a Brave Thinking mindset to every task.

Beginning with baby steps

Use this activation process as often as needed. Whatever steps you choose, do at least one five-minute "baby step" each day to fully invest in the development of your dream. Be humble to the ideas that come your way because the

Infinite offers ideas based on your readiness to receive them. The more you repeat this exercise, the stronger your results become. My son John didn't go to the plot of land where he wanted to build his dream home in Mexico just once. He visited every day, even if only for a few minutes.

My daughter, Jennifer Jiménez, began using the Brave Thinking Activation Process many years ago, at a difficult time in her life. A former professional dancer, she was accustomed to expressing herself creatively. But she found herself working long hours at a sales job, sitting all day in a tiny cubicle under fluorescent lights, smiling and dialing, where the only thing that moved was her mouth. "I felt like my work was meaningless," she said. No matter how hard she and her husband worked, the family struggled, and the stress and exhaustion infiltrated every part of her life. Instead of playing with her three small children, she snapped at them. "I felt scared," she said. "I didn't have a solution." Sleep deprived, she no longer had the energy to dance, do yoga, or even go on walks.

I invited Jennifer to attend one of my seminars. When encouraged to use the Brave Thinking Tool "What would I love?" she became irritated. "I can barely get through the week," she said. A life she would love sounded like a fairy tale.

I repeated to her the words that, many years ago, the visiting hospital chaplain spoke to a scared teenage mother the night before kidney surgery: "Just leave one corner of your mind open to the possibility." Jennifer agreed to that. Then I added, "If you're having a hard time believing in this, then believe in my belief." When we feel defeated, borrowing another person's belief can help provide the fortitude to persevere.

As Jennifer crafted a vision statement for a life she would love in all four quadrants, she wondered for the first time, "What if it could be easy?" After bringing her longings and discontent to the surface and envisioning herself living a dream that had already happened, she realized she couldn't go back to her old life. She was determined not to think the same thoughts and repeat the same actions that had kept her stuck.

Following a year of practice and study, Jennifer's life was completely transformed. She used the Brave Thinking Activation Process to ask intelligent questions of the Infinite. One of the first ideas she acted on was to create a prenatal dance video, setting her on a new path that led her to quit the job she loathed for one she loved. Jennifer traded her cubicle for a dance and yoga studio, starting a health and well-being business that incorporated movement and spiritual practices. She called the studio a "command center" for her soul. Dancing every day was part of her work, and her health improved. "The new vibration I was in made me feel healthy, strong, and radiant," she said. She doubled her income while working fewer hours. "I felt like my work was meaningful for the first time in a really, really long time," she said. "And my soul felt alive."

She was living abundantly in all four quadrants of her life. She became fully engaged with her children, reading to them and going on what she called "mommy dates" to ride go-carts or play miniature golf. "I played with them and loved them in the ways that they truly deserved," she said. Whereas mundane tasks such as laundry, cleaning, and driving the kids to appointments had once exhausted her, she now went about these ordinary activities in a spirit of joy. "I had a new, empowering paradigm about what motherhood could be," she said. "I was filling my cup." Jennifer and her husband also grew closer. "We fell even deeper in love with each other," she said.

Today, Jennifer is the director of the Brave Thinking Institute's health and well-being division, where she supports clients in building the kind of momentum she had for her own dream and teaches a kind of movement modality that promotes healing and well-being, one she invented.

Few of us become interested in transformation without a prompt. And for many, that trigger is pain. My awakening began with a life-threatening kidney disease. Jennifer was so emotionally depleted that she barely got through each week.

Tony Bodoh's prompt was anaphylactic shock. Married with two little girls he adored, Tony made an excellent living as a high-level analyst in a large corporation. But his health was eroding dangerously. Tony attended one of my seminars and told me that, in the previous year, he had wound up in the hospital needing urgent medical care three times after going into anaphylactic shock. This potentially life-threatening allergic reaction causes the heart to palpitate and the airways to narrow, blocking normal breathing. Doctors had put him through multiple tests, but none could identify the source of his allergic response.

We began to look at Tony's life to identify the areas where he didn't feel fully alive. Tony told me that although he initially loved his job, the situation had changed. The office environment had become toxic. Leadership treated staff poorly, and relationships between employees followed suit. Tony said, "Frankly, I feel like I need to check my soul at the door, go in and do my work, and then come back, try to find my soul, pick it up, and take it home with me."

Then he blurted out, "I wonder if I'm allergic to my job."

I asked what he would love doing, but as often happens, his initial response was to resist his own dream. Tony said he would love to start his own business, consulting with different corporations, and to have a team that supported him. But he also worried about supporting his family and how he would make his dream happen.

Tony was willing to put the "how" on hold. Using Brave Thinking Tools, he imagined himself living in his dream business. Staying true to the process, he generated inspired ideas about how to get his business started, one of which was to make his current employer a client—a contract he then secured.

The anaphylactic episodes ceased.

Today, he is the chief experience officer at Tony Bodoh International, a company whose mission is to "inspire and empower entrepreneurs to create businesses that transform lives and the world." He is also a bestselling author and podcast host.

With reverence for divine ideas

In this moment, you are standing at a crossroads, that sacred space between where you are and where you are headed. Pause to think about what influences your results. Your thoughts generate feelings, those feelings generate actions, and those actions generate your results. The ideas brought forth through the Brave Thinking Activation Process contain an element of the divine and, as such, are treated with reverence. Your brain is the interface between the finite and Infinite side of your nature. This beautiful piece of equipment gives us the ability to transact with the Infinite—and you are *always* transacting with the Infinite.

The only thing that changes is your awareness of how you transact.

Imagine owning a computer but not being aware that the Internet exists. The Internet stores and makes searchable almost all the information that humans have ever learned. You have access to all of it. But if you are unaware of the Internet, all you can access is the files on your computer. You don't use your equipment to its full potential. And that's how most people think. They don't go "online" and access the Infinite, the Higher Power that is always available to them. Once you learn what is out there, your ability to transact with information expands. All this has a magnetic charge: the universe's electrons organize and pull patterns together that, in turn, attract everything that looks like coincidences and accidents to us. Most people don't access the power that is available to them. They believe their lives will change once their circumstances do. "Once I get that promotion, we can finally take the vacation we've always wanted." "Once I meet my soulmate, then I will be happy."

In truth, Brave Thinking is just the opposite. Once you learn that you have access to a mind that knows *all* things, your ability to transact with greater insight and information expands. All this creates a magnetism. The forces of the universe come together to attract what we are in harmony with and have chosen to focus on and create. Brave Thinkers like you come from their vision rather than living solely in their circumstances.

Henry David Thoreau began, "I have learned this, at least, by my *experiment*" (my emphasis). Thoreau was willing to experiment, meaning he was open to trying something and failing. He didn't mind being wrong. No true scientist does;

a failure is just more data. The scientific method is a constant process of trial and error. Brave Thinking has been your invitation to conduct an experiment with your life, to care enough about this one precious life of yours to unlock your true power and potential for change and growth. In whatever form your dream may manifest, know that the discoveries you make through this experiment with your life will continue to unfold and yield even greater results.

ACTIVATING BRAVE THINKING

Brave Thinking Tool: Brave Thinking Activation Process
This process provides a system to tap into inspired insight and create an action plan for your dream.

Teaching points
- Source: Begin with a highly calibrated question to move toward your dream and jot down all the ideas that come to you—even if some seem preposterous.

- Sort: Identify those ideas from your list that make you feel expansive.

- Select: List your ideas in the order you will act on them.

- Schedule: Block out time on your calendar to pursue your selected ideas, making an appointment with your dream.

- Serve: Honor your commitment by following through on your scheduled tasks, treating each one with reverence.

Conclusion

BECOMING

"Every step in the right direction and every breath along the way becomes the realization of your dream. Your dream does not take you away from the present; on the contrary, your dream becomes reality in the present moment."

THICH NHAT HANH

The dream's not the prize.

The prize is who you become

As you move toward it.

YOU HAVE FOLLOWED all the steps to building a dream for a life you love, but your journey isn't over yet. The real magic of Brave Thinking requires one more step: *Becoming*. The person you become in the process of Brave Thinking is greater than the dream itself. The diligence, devotion, and daring that moved you outside your comfort zone has created an expanded version of you. Somewhere in the process of that hard work, you recognized a greater meaning. In building the tangible portion of your dream, you developed intangible, deeper qualities, such as increased awareness and aliveness. You recognized that you were never on this journey alone. Your realized dream is the brilliant product of your cocreation with the Infinite.

The realization of your dream rewards you with something greater than the home, career, or relationship that you originally envisioned. Behind this dream awaits a more expansive one, because life is always reaching for a more expanded expression of itself, like a blade of grass that presses through the cement, seeking light. Living in this grander scheme, you will take on an even more magnificent dream. This expanded view opens you to a vision unimaginable at an earlier stage. You can then vigorously pursue the new dream and once more grow into a greater version of your authentic self. As this pattern repeats, you discover that there is no separation between yourself and what you dream.

You thought you were building a dream.

In fact, the dream was building you.

What does it mean to "become"? Many years ago, I had the privilege of standing on the stage of the United Nations, along with Mohandas Gandhi's grandson and Martin Luther King Jr.'s children, as we launched Season for Nonviolence. This event is an annual sixty-four-day grassroots awareness campaign that honors the lives of two great men who spent their lives promoting peace through nonviolent means and were themselves assassinated. Gandhi's grandson Arun shared that his grandfather's most oft-repeated quote, "Be the change you want to see in the world," does not precisely represent what he said or intended. Gandhi understood how words form reality. What he said was "*Become* the change you want to see in the world." "Be" is powerful, but finite. On the deepest level, Gandhi understood that transformation is not a mere moment, but a lifelong process. "Be" implies that having achieved what you set out to accomplish, your mission is complete.

Brave Thinkers do not cross the finish line and call it good. They are grateful for the good, yet remain ever-evolving, ever becoming.

Brave Thinkers enter what I call "the field of impact." That is, the dream becomes more than a physical manifestation of their desire. Your dream can profoundly affect every aspect of your life and the lives of those around you. You are not the same person as the one who was once hemmed in by circumstances and limited by Common-Hour Thinking. You reached the edge of who you knew yourself to be and stepped beyond to find that you contained far more than you knew. The greatest impact comes not from achieving your dream but from awakening to the person you are becoming. As you listen to the still, small voice and pursue your dream for higher good, spiritual gifts unfold like surprise presents. These gifts, which far exceed your original vision, allow you to find pleasure and joy in all that surrounds you. The person you evolve into as you build your dream through the struggles, victories, and disappointments— that is the true dream. Your evolution can begin at any age and knows no bounds. You thought you were building a dream. In fact, the dream was building you.

When everything fell apart for me years ago—losing the church, my livelihood, and my reputation—I had to face the reality that my old life was gone. My letting go left claw marks as I felt dragged from the dream that I had spent more than two decades building. Now, it was time for something new. As I followed the process detailed in this book, I realized something. Had my previous life proceeded as planned, I'd still be there, and "there" was a very constricted version of my present life. I realized that who

I had become by going through this process, pain and all, was a far more aware and alive version of Mary.

There is a power breathing in you that is always greater than anything outside you. It took me years to accomplish my goal of paying back the millions of dollars in debt. I didn't walk away from the problem. I'm proud of honoring that commitment, but prouder still of who I became in the process. I used Brave Thinking not only to create a goal of a zero balance but to become a much better teacher. The crisis humbled me in a way that grew my sensitivity and compassion and deepened my understanding of how powerfully the Infinite can work in our lives. What I have learned and continue to learn through more than four decades of study and practice is a proven, reliable, and repeatable system of transformation that anybody can use.

Just as Thomas Edison didn't invent electricity, I didn't invent how transformation happens. I discovered and codified a simple system for working with the invisible laws that govern how all results occur. When you wire a house to code and hook it to a grid or solar panel, you can turn on the lights. And just like that correctly wired house, you can plug into this system of transformation at any time. If you follow this system, you will create more expansive results. That is inevitable. But even more than that, the greatest gift will be what you didn't even think to expect.

I found a simple way for others to transform their lives, and it has been my greatest honor to share this work with so many. Today, there are millions of people all over the world who are teaching and following this system I discovered, unlocking the power of Brave Thinking in their daily lives. But what touches me profoundly is knowing that they are becoming more of who they were created to be: ever-expanding versions of themselves.

Whatever the status of your dream at this moment, please know that what you have accomplished thus far exceeds the sum of your efforts. Your dream may be unfolding as you envisioned, or very differently. It may have taken an unexpected detour. Perhaps old paradigms have resurfaced, throwing you off course. You can honor your progress before your dream comes true. Sometimes, we can be so focused on the future that we miss the beauty available in the present moment. Just by incorporating a few of the Brave Thinking Tools in your life, you are already experiencing an increased sense of abundance. Rejoice at how far you have come, the obstacles you have surmounted, the fears you have befriended, or the feeling of gratitude that accompanies you through the day. As Ralph Waldo Emerson said, "The mind once stretched by a new idea never returns to its original dimensions." So it is with your life.

Shortly before my husband, Joe, and I were married, we both had events scheduled on the East Coast and decided to meet in Concord, Massachusetts, home to many of the great transcendentalists. We picnicked at Walden Pond, where Thoreau spent two years writing *Walden*. Joe and I took turns reading parts of Thoreau's treatise aloud to one another. When he started the passage I reference throughout this book, something new awakened in me. "I learned this, at least, by my experiment: that if one advances confidently in the direction of his dreams, and endeavors to live the life which he has imagined, he will meet with a success unexpected in common hours."

I realized these words are a code, a formula for how transformation occurs. I believe this passage is so beloved because we are wired for transformation in our souls. Most of us have no conscious awareness of how the Infinite works, but our soul knows. I had quoted this passage hundreds, if not thousands of times, but not until I sat in the place where Thoreau sat, immersed in the sheer energy of this magical setting, did the deeper meaning materialize for me. I believe that the energy of places where great leaders and thinkers lived and congregated, where individuals made a stand for freedom and civil rights, are imbued with the essence of what occurred there. My experience at Walden Pond planted the seed of an idea in my head.

Years later, I began leading retreats to these very places. Tiffany Neuman is a client who joined me on one such pilgrimage to Concord, where she and others immersed themselves in the philosophy of the great transcendental-ist philosophers, including Emerson and Thoreau. I met Tiffany at an especially difficult time in her life. She had just ended a toxic relationship and had gained sixty pounds during college. She had undergone three surgeries, which culminated in the doctor telling her, "You're never going to have children." Tiffany had long dreamed of being a cre-ative director and worked in the industry, but as a graphic designer. After the toxic relationship and with grief over her infertility and health issues, she doubted herself and her talent. "I really felt like my dream wasn't going to happen," she said. "I felt stuck and scared."

Tiffany attended one of my seminars, where she cre-ated a vibrant four-quadrant vision statement that put her health first. "I am healthy, vibrant, fit, and feel amazing on a daily basis," she wrote. She signed up to run a marathon. At the time, she said, "I couldn't even run a mile." But she began walking regularly, then jogging. She joined a team that supported her progress, especially so her Saturday running partner.

Tiffany lost weight, finished the marathon, and wound up marrying her running partner. Like all Brave Thinkers, she recognized herself as ever-evolving and becoming, and she continued to move in the direction of her dreams. She became a successful creative director and eventually started her own business. One dream, however, remained elusive, but Tiffany always held out a spark of hope. As I mentioned, she joined a retreat to Concord, where she was inspired by the great thinkers in this birthplace of transcendentalism, a movement that recognizes the divine in everyday life.

When her dream baby was born, Tiffany named her Emerson.

A Formula to Transform Your Life

Henry David Thoreau spent his life studying spirituality and concluded his greatest work with the wisdom gained from his sojourn at Walden Pond. As you look once again at his words, can you see how this formula will transform your own life?

> "I learned this, at least, by my experiment: that if one advances confidently in the direction of his dreams..."

Without a new direction, our minds default to creating what they always have. That's why we *advance confidently in the direction of our dreams*.

Brave Thinkers confidently commit themselves to the daily practice of dream-building, weaving the tools into their hearts and minds like muscle memory.

Deep inside you is a dream for an extraordinary life. You were put on this planet to achieve your dreams. Notice and honor the discontent stirring deep in your soul. Respect the feeling that is nudging you toward a greater experience, telling you, "I'm glad you're restless. Don't settle for a little life." Creating new results requires learning to partner with the Infinite, the energy that exists everywhere and guides us to produce something we truly desire. Instead of settling for mediocrity, Brave Thinkers like David Norris confidently commit themselves to the daily practice of dream-building, weaving the tools into their hearts and minds like muscle memory. David listened to his longings, leaving a successful banking career and relentless migraines to start his own consulting business, which has given him far more time to spend with his granddaughters. "What matters most is that I get to serve as a living example to these girls so that they can grow up and be who they want to be," David says. "And that gives *me* life."

"*. . . And endeavors to live the life which he has imagined, he will meet with a success unexpected in common hours.*"

The Infinite has given you the power to imagine. You can create the same life with different pictures to it year after year, or you can carefully and vividly and distinctly imagine a life you would love. Being specific about your dream allows you to see a picture of this life, one you can literally and energetically step inside. Start with what you want, and then envision it having already happened. Boldly ask yourself, "What would I love?" Then put the "how" on hold. This success is your birthright, one you cannot plan.

Concerned about supporting his family, Tony Bodoh hesitated to give up his job, even though he suspected it may have contributed to several episodes of life-threatening anaphylactic shock. Then he boldly stepped into his dream of owning his own business. He has more time for his family and hasn't experienced anaphylactic shock in years.

"He will put some things behind..."

Resentment or hurt dwells somewhere in the mind of every person. Holding a grudge punishes the person who betrayed us—or so we'd like to think. But the truth is, every relationship is an invitation to experience a more expansive life. Forgiveness frees. Brave Thinking requires us to open our heart at the very moment every instinct tells us to shut it down. At the most profound level, those who have hurt us the most can offer the greatest gifts. For Lauren Brollier Newton, forgiveness was a gift she gave herself. Lauren was newly married to a man who led a double life and frequently ignored and belittled his bride. By steadfastly practicing forgiveness, Lauren became grateful to her former husband for letting her go. Freed from resentment, she turned up the volume on her visions for love and a career. Today, she is happily married to the man of her dreams and growing her work into a seven-figure business.

"... Will pass an invisible boundary..."

Fear is part of the human condition. Fear of loneliness, fear of getting old, fear of failure—even the most successful among us encounter every one of these. As Brave Thinkers you recognize and acknowledge fear as part of the dream-building journey. Rather than attempting to rid yourself of fear, you acknowledge its presence, confident that you have a far more powerful companion in the Infinite. When something seemingly bad happens, instead of panicking, you pause and give yourself three days to look for the good. By training yourself how to feel fear and still move toward your dream, you pass an invisible boundary, bringing you closer to a life you would truly love. When Bill Harris was sued for $1 million, he wrote out a list of all the possible good in this seemingly miserable situation. In that expansive mindset, he documented how he had developed his business, sent the documentation to the person suing him, and the lawsuit disappeared. Drowning in debt, Kim Luret spent years living in fear that her family would be evicted again, or that the electricity, phone, or both would be cut off once more. Today, Kim owns her own successful business, is married to her soulmate, and says she lives "almost every moment in calm, peace, and joy."

*"New, universal, and more liberal laws will begin
to establish themselves around and within
him; or the old laws be expanded, and interpreted
in his favor in a more liberal sense, and he will live
with the license of a higher order of beings."*

The universe bestows the good things of life in proportion to a person's readiness to receive. Practicing gratitude shows us that we have more resources than we think, and that we are capable of more than we believe. When you live in a state of generative gratitude, more opportunities avail themselves to you, and you have a more expansive experience of being alive. Practicing gratitude fortifies our dreams, drawing even greater good to us, because gratitude is harmonious with abundance. As you replenish the world around you with your time, talent, and treasure, you move forward. As you circulate your good and move toward your dream with a giving heart, you feel as if new universal laws are at work for you. You step into the freely given abundance of the universe, becoming a person of increase, as Benny Vaughn did. A person of increase consciously touches the lives of others. Benny's dream is to build an athletic training facility for young people who have challenges, helping them to recognize their inherent worth. Brave Thinking Tools "made a dramatic impact on my life," Benny said, "helping me to realize why I'm here, and that is to help others."

*"In proportion as he simplifies his life, the
laws of the universe will appear less complex..."*

As you move into your dream, you may feel as if you are stepping out onto thin air. But you are not alone. The still, small voice of inspired insight exists in each one of us. You simplify your life by distinguishing that voice from all the chatter in your mind, all the doubts, fears, and voices of insecurity. Wisdom from the Infinite will lead you in your decisions that produce extraordinary results. This calm inner voice, the trusted voice of guidance will never berate or shame you. Instead, it persistently nudges you in the direction of your highest good. As you follow your guidance, the laws of the universe no longer seem so confounding. You feel empowered to take the next step. The more we listen, the louder and more resonant our still, small voice grows, as my son Mat Boggs discovered on the eve of his application to medical school. Mat changed his life trajectory by listening to his still, small voice, which was guiding him to become a teacher, not a doctor. By heeding that voice, Mat cowrote a bestselling book that landed him on the *Today Show* and in an international career in speaking, teaching, and coaching.

> *". . . And solitude will not be solitude, nor*
> *poverty poverty, nor weakness weakness."*

Paradigms are a collection of assumptions and beliefs that determine how you see the world. An unhealthy paradigm knows everything about you: your failed attempts, forgotten dreams, and unrealized goals. Whatever image your mind clings to tends to replicate itself in your real world. When you try to grow, a negative paradigm will seek to pull you back, thwarting your efforts. When you speak the truth of the life you would love and hold that vision, your paradigms begin to shift. If you long for a loving relationship and start expressing love right where you are, you cannot help but attract other loving people to your life. Your *solitude will not be solitude.* Jubril Wilson is a Brave Thinker who once called himself a loser. His paradigms told him, "You're not a real man. You're not a good father." Today, Jubril is a successful real estate broker, happily married and close to his daughter. By taking the courageous step to challenge paradigms that had left him barely surviving, Jubril says he has "realized dreams I couldn't even have imagined."

> *"If you have built castles in the air, your work*
> *need not be lost; that is where they should be . . ."*

All dream builders experience failure. They spend a portion of their lives building castles whose drawbridge they will never cross. If what you desire never comes to pass, or if your dream manifests only to crumble later, as mine did, take heart. In each adversity is planted the seed of a greater good. The Infinite has not abandoned you. As you stand for better over bitter, you find that it is your very failures that can propel you toward a higher level of awareness and success.

When the dream I had spent more than two decades building collapsed, I was devastated. Ultimately, my crisis paved the way for a far more expansive life and made me a better teacher. The Brave Thinking Institute I founded has made it possible to help far more people to build their dreams. My teaching and coaching philosophies now serve individuals in ninety-two countries around the world. Today, I also have the privilege and honor of working with my four adult children. Each of them created their own businesses and were successful in their own right. One by one, they decided to help our clients create meaningful results with the very transformation they had studied and experienced personally. And every day I am grateful for the unexpected dream that brought my husband, Joe Dickey, into my life. He is the soulmate for whom I have always longed.

"Now put the foundations under them."

We put foundations under our dreams and make them real one step at a time, finding that we, too, have joined the ranks of the great Brave Thinkers. I encourage you to say, "This or something better." That attitude gives room for the Infinite to grow a greater dream in you, a dream that you cannot see from where you stand now. Keep moving vigorously in the direction of your dream. As each new dream comes to pass or falls by the wayside, you continue to grow. Reserve a miracle zone in your mind, a place where no disbelief can mar your vision. "I don't know how my dream will happen, but I know it can happen. I believe that the power of the Infinite is greater than any problem I face. I'm going to challenge the belief that I am limited by my bank account, education, or past failures. I'm going to reserve a corner of my mind for pure possibility and savor every moment, embracing it as a new possibility."

The Long Walk Is Part of the Gift

A teacher who had gone to Africa with the Peace Corps was given a beautiful seashell by one of her students, a young man who had appreciated her teaching. But the teacher was a little confused. The ocean was miles away across rocky terrain. There were no cars in the remote village where her student lived. "Where did you find this?" she asked. "Did a trader bring it to your village?"

"No," he said, explaining that he walked to the coast to find it.

"You went all that way to bring me a seashell. Thank you!" She could only imagine how many hours the journey had taken.

"Yes," he acknowledged. "The long walk was part of the gift."

Dream-building is a long walk for most of us, one that requires you to step outside your comfort zone. Undertaking this journey not only brings reality to your dream, it empowers you to give a gift to the world that comes from your expanded capacity to receive and give abundantly. The dreams we build on earth are temporary, but the transformation in our soul is everlasting. Your long walk—the process—is part of your gift.

So now, dear reader, I leave this magnificent system of transformation in your hands and heart. Love your life, love your dreams, and practice Brave Thinking. You will forever be glad you did.

Acknowledgments

I WANT FIRST TO thank the two main mentors in my life, Jack Boland and Bob Proctor, who helped me discover the science behind transformation and how to bring it into my life and others' lives. Although they are both gone now, I hear their wisdom in my mind and heart daily.

Thank you to the many congregants and clients who, over the years, experimented with the Brave Thinking system in their own lives. They proved to me this system not only works but it works *every* time it is executed exactly.

Thank you to Christy Scattarella, Blaine Dickey, and Jeff Goins for your help in bringing this book to life. Your talent and gifts are in every page.

Thank you to my dearest and longest friend, Colleen Schuerlein, who in 1969 agreed to be my lifelong companion in our transformations along the journey of life. Your love, support, and wisdom has been a bedrock for me for over fifty-four years as of this book's release.

Thank you to my other wonderfully aware and brilliant friends in the journey of discovering how transformation occurs: Debbie Tallman, Cynthia Kersey and Blaine

Bartlett, Sheila and Marcus Gillette, Kim Luret, and Vince Czaplyski.

Thank you to Kirsten Welles. Your friendship, wisdom, and insight has been seminal in the work we do in helping people live lives they love.

Thank you to my amazing "bonus children": Jennifer Barnes, Blaine and Bridges Dickey, and Michael and Matthew Morrissey, you are all gifted and wonderful in your own and unique ways. I will always be grateful for your accepting me into your lives, cocreating a wonderful blended family, and for the deep love and great fun we share.

Thank you to my four wonderful "birth children": John Boggs, Rich Boggs, Jennifer Jiménez, and Mathew Boggs. You four have been prime examples of what applied Brave Thinking produces in dreams coming true, not only for you, but for your terrific spouses and children, as well. Thank you for the success you each earned and manifested in your more than twenty years of experience in the world of business. You brought all that learning and your awareness in Brave Thinking and joined me in the cocreation of Brave Thinking Institute. You have each, along with me, dedicated your lives to helping people all over the world in overcoming their deepest challenges and building their greatest dreams.

I've saved the best for last.

To the man who has believed in me every step of the way since our meeting in 2005, the man who helped me form, start, and build Brave Thinking Institute, my husband and self-proclaimed "second most interesting man in the world," Joe Dickey.

You had done your own study in transformation long before we met. You brought your wisdom, guidance, and unwavering support, believing that as we applied this Brave Thinking system, we could reduce that immense debt to a zero balance all the while creating work that truly helped each person whom we had the privilege of serving.

For your daily, steadfast support, and for your guidance, know that your contribution to my life and to this work is immeasurable.

One more deep gratitude: It was you who held the vision of a truly connected life, a blended family that embraces all our kids, their spouses, and our grandchildren.

Your steadfastness in holding this dream, beyond circumstances in the beginning, paved a solid path that we all travel together.

What a great and truly loving family we all enjoy today. Yes, everyone has done their part. But you, my love, led the way.

You will forever be THE *most interesting man* in the world to me.

About the Author

RICHARD LUU

MARY MORRISSEY is widely considered the world's foremost expert on "dream-building"—the art and science of transforming your dreams into reality. Morrissey started studying transformation in 1971 and has been teaching transformation since 1981. She is the author of two best-selling books, *No Less Than Greatness* and *Building Your Field of Dreams*, the latter of which became a PBS special. She has addressed the United Nations three times and was invited to co-convene three different week-long meetings with His Holiness the Dalai Lama. She also met with President Nelson Mandela in Cape Town, South Africa, to address some of the most significant issues that our world faces.

Through her work and founding the Brave Thinking Institute, Morrissey has empowered millions of people worldwide to achieve new heights of spiritual aliveness, prosperity, and authentic success.

She lives in California with her husband, Joe Dickey, and their dog, Molly.

About Brave Thinking® Institute

B RAVE THINKING INSTITUTE'S mission is to empower
people to create and live a life they love.

Whether it's developing awareness of spiritual principles, feeling a sense of deep purpose and meaning, creating vibrant health, finding love, deepening relationships,
succeeding in business, or serving others as a coach—
whatever the dream is, the Brave Thinking Institute is the
premier training center for transformational coaching!

Learn more about our digital programs, events, master-
minds, and retreats by visiting bravethinkinginstitute.com.

ADDITIONAL BRAVE THINKING RESOURCES

You now understand the art and science of designing a dream and turning that dream into reality. If you'd love support in going from *understanding* these transformational principles to *mastering* them, so you can build any dream quickly, Brave Thinking Institute is here to help beyond the pages of this book!

"Designing a Life You Love" Guided Meditation Bundle

Clarify your dreams. Craft a beautiful vision of a life you'd love. Tune in to that vision frequently with this free guided audio meditation bundle. Visit **bravethinkingbook.com/meditation**.

"100 Common-Hour Thoughts and How to Transform Them" Kit

Reprogram your mind to shift from Common-Hour Thinking to Brave Thinking, with this free kit. As you do, you will quickly begin experiencing a more expansive life.
Visit **bravethinkingbook.com/thoughts**.

"Winning the Battles of the Mind" Affirmation Collection

Stay connected to your strength, especially during those moments you need a boost of confidence that you are greater than any circumstance, situation, or condition.
Visit **bravethinkingbook.com/affirmations**.

For access to the free resources above plus other bonus Brave Thinking Tools, visit **bravethinkingbook.com/resources** now.

Remember, think bravely, act boldly, and live a life you love!

BRAVE THINKING® INSTITUTE

THINK **BRAVELY,**
ACT **BOLDLY** &
LIVE A LIFE YOU **LOVE!**